THE MURDERED DEAD SPEAK

The Murdered Dead Speak

Book I: The Haystack Murder

SHIRLEY SMOLKO

Cavallaro Publishing

CONTENTS

COPYRIGHT NOTICE

Cover Design by Shirley Smolko

Printed in the U.S.A.

First Printing 2023

Print Book ISBN: 978-1-958104-07-1

Library of Congress Control Number: 2023921270

Cavallaro Publishing

North Venice, FL

DEDICATION

To Joe, my husband, and Ernest Hemingway, my writing guide: Many thanks for encouraging me to write.

There was a day when I had been praying and seeking guidance from the Creator as to whether or not I should continue writing. On the night of this day, my husband dreamed he was having a cocktail with Ernest Hemingway at Sloppy Joe's. In the dream, he asked Mr. Hemingway, "Do you have any advice for my wife?" Ernest took a swig of his drink, turned his head, looked at Joe, and said, "Tell Shirl to keep at it." The next morning, we woke up facing each other in bed. Joe looked me directly in the eyes and said, "I have a message from Ernest Hemingway; he said for you to keep at it."

Now this wouldn't normally have been a big deal for me; however, because my husband didn't know I had prayed the day before for guidance as to whether or not I should continue writing, it was definitely a big deal. It was a concrete answer to prayer. So, once again, here I go. I'm gonna keep at it!

PREFACE

My husband and I had planned a day trip to Ybor City in Tampa, FL., to do some touring and take in the essence of this exciting little Latin City within a city. A few days before embarking on our trip, I had a dream one night in which I was transported to another time and place to witness the life and murder of a very kind and successful cigar manufacturer whose death had been misclassified as a suicide. The day after my dream, research for our planned trip put a name to the kindly man—Blas Trujillos.

This dream made me wonder about other souls who were victims of murders that were either unsolved, misclassified, or wrongly adjudicated. I did an internet search and found a list of names of murder victims going back several centuries. As I scrolled down the list, I began to see visions of those victims who were reaching out to me. As the visions flashed before my eyes, I knew I had to tell their stories. However, out of the utmost respect for the privacy and compassion for the enduring pain of the families left behind by more recent victims, I made a heart-wrenching decision to confine the stories within this book series to those souls whose tragic fates had been consigned to the distant echoes of the 19th and early twentieth centuries. It was a choice that struck a balance between unveiling the truth and safeguarding the tender wounds of the present.

As a psychic medium, my role is to bridge the gap between the physical world and the spiritual realm. I'm often asked how it's possible for a spirit to tell their story through me. I'll try to explain the process and the various psychic abilities that come into play during my communication with spirits.

One fundamental aspect of being a psychic medium is having heightened sensitivity to energy vibrations. In their energetic form, spirits emit signals or frequencies into the spiritual realm. It's akin to tuning in to a specific radio station to pick up their signal.

When a spirit wishes to communicate, it sends out a call into the spiritual realm. This call is usually directed at a medium they know will come in contact with the individual(s) the message is intended for.

As a medium, I receive impressions from spirits using various psychic senses. These impressions can manifest in different ways:

- Clairvoyance (Clear Seeing): I might see mental images or scenes related to the spirit's story. Most of the time, these images play out like a movie in my mind's eye. This is one of the core abilities I used in writing this book.

- Clairaudience (Clear Hearing): Messages or words may be spoken to me audibly in my mind. Sometimes, I will be given a message through the lyrics of a song that the spirit plays in my head. Usually, I am given whole sentences or a continuous dialogue of conversation, such as "I must be leaving now. Tell Nora not to worry. Gina will be okay." This is another core ability I used to write this book.

- Clairsentience (Clear Feeling): I might experience the emotions and physical sensations associated with the spirit's death. This psychic ability helps me understand the emotions they were feeling at the time of death, such as fear or regret. Most of the spirits that come to me, communicate the way they died by making me feel their pain or symptoms, such as head pain, chest pain, or symptoms of a respiratory problem. This is a core ability I used to write this book.

• Claircognizance (Clear Knowing): Claircognizance involves a psychic medium receiving intuitive knowledge or insights about the spirit's story without any logical explanation. I might suddenly "know" information about a spirit's personality, life, or message. Spirits can share their story by directly influencing my thoughts and understanding, allowing me to access and communicate their knowledge. I used this ability often in writing this book.

• Clairalience (Clear Smelling) and Clairgustance (Clear Tasting): These abilities involve smelling odors or tasting flavors that are associated with the spirit's story. For example, I might experience the smell of a discharged firearm or the metallic taste of blood in my mouth, which helps me to understand a spirit's message of how they were murdered. I used this ability often in writing this book.

• Psychometry: Psychometry is the ability to gain information about an object by touching or holding it. There have been times when I used this ability to receive impressions; however, it is not really helpful in writing a book.

• Automatic Writing and Drawing: Some mediums may use automatic writing or drawing to allow the spirit to guide their hand, creating written messages or drawings that convey the spirit's story or messages. I sometimes use automatic writing when trying to string words and sentences in general writing. Mostly, I rely on what I'm seeing, hearing, feeling, smelling, or tasting when I'm communicating with spirit. However, I believe automatic writing helps me get my impressions carried over onto paper. In the last few years, I have been made aware that Ernest Hemingway is my writing guide. As noted in my acknowledgment, Ernest came to my husband in a dream and told him to tell me to, "Keep at it!" My husband had no idea that I had asked God the day before for guidance as to whether or not I should continue writing.

To sum it up, a spirit can tell its story through me using my psychic abilities as a channel of communication. I act as a receptor, receiving the information conveyed by the spirit through these different psychic senses, which can provide a rich and detailed narrative of the spirit's personality, experiences, and messages.

Shirley Smolko

September 2023

~ 1 ~

INTRODUCTION

This edition of *The Murdered Dead Speak* delves into the haunting true story of Sarah Maria Cornell, a young woman whose life took a tragic turn in 1832, leaving an indelible mark on the history of Tiverton, RI. Set against the backdrop of the early 19th, century in a quiet New England town, this chilling narrative explores the dark and mysterious circumstances surrounding her brutal murder.

I have reopened this long-closed case, inviting readers to join me in my relentless quest for answers and the pursuit of justice for Sarah Maria Cornell. I am not alone in my mission; the murdered spirit of Sarah rises from the grave to assist me, guiding me on an otherworldly journey to reveal concealed truths.

Chapter two delves into the mysterious circumstances surrounding the death of Sarah Maria Cornell, a young woman whose life came to a tragic end on the evening of December 20, 1832, in Tiverton, Rhode Island. Found by Farmer John Durfee in a haunting tableau near a haystack, Sarah's demise raises questions that echo through time. The preliminary case file unveils a complex narrative, inter-twining elements of despair, scandal, and a curious twist of fate. As the details unfold—from the initial shock of discovery to the somber decision of a jury—the enigma of Sarah Cornell's demise emerges, leaving investigators and onlookers grappling with the haunting question: Was it suicide?

Chapter three dives into the chilling aftermath of S. M. Cornell's death as the coroner's jury reconvenes to hear testimonies and examine the gruesome details of her post-mortem examination. Dr. Foster Hooper paints a vivid picture of the injuries on the body, igniting whispers of murder among the onlookers. The revelation of a mysterious slip of paper, pointing fingers at Rev. Mr. Avery, intensifies the suspense. As the crowd reacts with shock and anger, the coroner unveils incriminating letters that further implicate the accused. The once-considered suicide takes a dark turn, leading the jury to a verdict that not only questions the cause of S. M. Cornell's death but also places suspicion squarely on the shoulders of Rev. E. K. Avery. The chapter unfolds with a growing sense of mystery, scandal, and public outrage in the wake of a possible murder.

Chapter four thrusts us into a tumultuous Sunday, usually serene in Puritanical New England, but marred by the exceptional events following the death of Sarah Maria Cornell. As the coroner's jury contemplates a suicide verdict, public opinion vehemently declares murder, heightening the already fervent atmosphere. Rev. Ephraim K. Avery, a once-revered preacher, finds himself accused, challenging the unwavering faith of those who idolized him. The chapter unravels a web of societal tensions—religious, anti-religious, and class-based—further fueled by the deceased's working-class background. The formation of a Vigilance Committee underscores the public's thirst for justice, leading to intense confrontations and demands for Avery's surrender. With mounting evidence against him, including damning testimonies and an attempted abortion revelation, Avery's fate appears sealed, and the chapter closes with the specter of justice looming over him.

Chapter Five delves into the tragic story of Sarah Maria Cornell, tracing her roots in the quaint town of Rupert, Vermont, where her life began on May 3, 1803. Known for her piety, truthfulness, and religious fervor from a young age, Sarah, affectionately called Sally, entered the cotton industry early to support her family. Despite her beauty and devout nature, she struggled to find a suitable companion until her encounter with Rev. Ephraim K. Avery, a charismatic preacher she admired like a demi-god. The chapter unveils the evolution of their relationship, starting innocently with ordinary pastor-parishioner interactions. However, in August, at a camp meeting near Providence, Rhode Island, Avery's manipulative tactics ensnare Sarah. The narrative takes a dark turn as Avery exploits her admiration, leading to a betrayal of trust and the degradation of Sarah's honor. The chapter unfolds the painful events that transpired that night, revealing the sinister side of the revered preacher and the helpless plight of a young woman ensnared by his deceit.

In the unfolding drama of Sarah's life, Chapter Six marks a pivotal moment as she grapples with the consequences of a betrayal that threatens to shatter her world. Living with her brother-in-law, Grindall Rawson, and assisting in his tailor shop, Sarah's demeanor reveals a hidden turmoil. The revelation of her predicament, a result of a liaison with Mr. Avery, sets off a chain of events that propels her to Fall River, where she must confront the complexities of her situation. As the stars illuminate the New England Indian Summer night, Sarah embarks on a fateful meeting with the man who has altered the course of her life. The chapter unfolds with tension and emotion, setting the stage for the challenges that lie ahead for Sarah in the face of societal expectations and personal turmoil

In the grim chronicles of Sarah Cornell's tragic tale, Chapter Seven unfolds with a foreboding title—The Fatal Day. The narrative takes a sinister turn as Sarah, residing with the Hathaway family, receives a chilling letter from Mr. Avery, setting the stage for a catastrophic rendezvous. As the shadows lengthen on the fateful afternoon, Sarah engages in seemingly mundane interactions, oblivious to the impending darkness. A whispered conversation reveals the haunting origin of her distress, rooted in a camp meeting at Thompson. The chapter meticulously details the events leading to that ominous December 20th evening, as Sarah, her demeanor strangely buoyant, departs for a rendezvous with Avery. The night unfolds with an eerie quiet, and the reader is plunged into a chilling scene where the macabre plans of the antagonist take a horrifying turn. The narrative crescendos with a ghastly tableau, leaving the reader to grapple with the aftermath of a deed most foul.

In the chilling aftermath of the murder, Chapter Eight, ominously titled "The Murderer Takes Flight," unveils the desperate escape of Mr. Avery. Fleeing the haystack crime scene, he charts a course toward Howland's Bridge, intent on reaching Portsmouth and then Bristol under the cover of darkness. The narrative weaves a tale of Avery's calculated actions, including the mysterious loss of his handkerchief, as he seeks refuge in the only hotel in Portsmouth run by Jeremiah Gilford. The cloak-and-dagger atmosphere intensifies as Avery's interactions with Gilford unfold, hinting at the fugitive's cunning and deceit. The chapter explores Avery's attempts to manipulate situations to his advantage, from fabricating a false preaching engagement to securing shelter for the night. As dawn breaks, Avery crosses the ferry, evading the suspicions of those around him. The reader is drawn into the tension of a man on the run, navigating a web of lies and leveraging his status to escape the clutches of justice. The narrative builds an unsettling backdrop of secret meetings, perjury, and the brewing discontent of a community grappling with the repercussions of a heinous crime. Avery's flight becomes a harrowing tale of deceit and evasion, setting the stage for the unfolding drama that awaits in the pursuit of justice.

In chapter nine, the narrative takes a riveting turn as the people of Fall River, outraged by Avery's flight, mobilize a determined party to hunt him down and bring him back to face the consequences of his alleged crime. Despite Avery's attempts at disguise, including shaving and cutting his hair, the relentless pursuit leads to his re-arrest. Discovered concealed in the house of Mr. Mayo, a prominent figure in the Methodist church, Avery contends that he cannot be arrested without a requisition. However, the pursuing party convinces him otherwise, setting the stage for his reluctant return to Rhode Island for trial. The chapter delves into the mounting evidence against Avery, with the exhumation and examination of the murdered girl's body revealing signs of an attempted abortion. As the government gains confidence in securing a conviction, the grand jury presents an indictment, paving the way for Avery's arrest and subsequent plea of not guilty. The unfolding drama captures the tension within the courtroom, with Avery's demeanor shifting from jaunty triumph to a more subdued apprehension. The chapter concludes with the commencement of the trial, marked by legal maneuvers, requests, and the meticulous selection of jurors, offering a foreboding glimpse into the unfolding courtroom drama. The narrative skillfully weaves together the intricate details of legal proceedings and the public's thirst for justice, setting the stage for a trial that will captivate the community and reverberate through the halls of justice.

In the enthralling Chapter 10, the narrative unfolds as the trial begins on Monday, May 6th, with Avery entering the courtroom, displaying a composed demeanor that belies the severity of the charges against him. The Clerk of Court introduces the legal combatants, revealing the formidable counsels enlisted for both the state and the defense. The proceedings commence with a motion from the Attorney General to proceed with the trial, setting the stage for the intense legal battles ahead.

The second day of the trial, on Tuesday, May 7th, witnesses the continuation of the proceedings, marked by the formal reading of the indictment against Avery. As each count detailing the heinous charges is presented, Avery maintains an outward composure, though subtle details betray the inner turmoil. The narrative masterfully captures the courtroom dynamics, emphasizing the gravity of the accusations against Avery and the meticulous legal procedures unfolding.

Moving to the third day of the trial, Wednesday, May 8th, the narrative delves into the challenges encountered in selecting an impartial jury. The complexities of jury selection become a focal point, with the defense expressing concerns and seeking alternative methods to ensure a fair trial. The court's rulings on jury selection practices add layers of intrigue to the unfolding legal saga, providing insight into the intricacies of the judicial process.

As the trial progresses, the reader is immersed in the unfolding drama, witnessing the meticulous assembly of a jury and the strategic maneuvers of the legal teams. The chapter concludes with the names of the selected jurors, offering a glimpse into the unique challenges faced during their selection. With the stage set for the trial to proceed, Chapter 10 promises a riveting exploration of the first, second, and third days of this gripping legal battle.

In Chapter 11, the courtroom is charged with anticipation as the trial enters its crucial phase. On the fourth day, the atmosphere in the courtroom is electric, with a diverse audience comprising both factory operatives from Fall River and members of Avery's church in Bristol. Dutee J. Pearce, Esq., the prosecutor, opens the case by emphasizing the gravity of the charges against Ephraim K. Avery— murder.

As Pearce lays out the prosecution's strategy, he promises to unveil a compelling narrative backed by evidence. The government's case hinges on proving that on December 21, 1832, Sarah Maria Cornell's lifeless body was discovered hanging near a haystack in Tiverton. Pearce meticulously outlines the timeline and circumstances surrounding Cornell's departure from Fall River, her alleged intimacy with Avery, and the suspicious events leading up to her tragic demise.

The narrative then seamlessly transitions to the testimonies presented by the prosecution witnesses. From John Durfee's discovery of the body to the intricate details of the knot around Cornell's neck, each witness contributes crucial pieces to the puzzle. The court hears from the coroner, Dr. Foster Hooper, and Dr. Thomas Wilbur, whose examinations hint at the possibility of foul play. The intricate web of evidence is further woven through testimonies from postmasters, eyewitnesses, and those who crossed paths with Avery on the fateful day.

The chapter builds suspense as it delves into the various facets of the prosecution's case, unraveling a complex narrative of events leading up to the alleged murder. The meticulous attention to detail, coupled with the diverse array of witness accounts, paints a vivid picture of the prosecution's argument. As the testimonies unfold, Chapter 11 promises to captivate readers with the intricacies of the case against Ephraim K. Avery, setting the stage for a gripping courtroom showdown.

In Chapter 12, as the trial marches into its seventh, eighth, and ninth days on Monday, May 13th, the courtroom remains a cauldron of anticipation, brimming with spectators eager for the unfolding drama. The accused, Ephraim K. Avery, perhaps a shade paler than at the trial's commencement, maintains his composed demeanor, seated near his counsel, absorbing the testimonies with undivided attention.

The proceedings kick off with the testimony of Horney Hornden, a member of the committee appointed by Fall River citizens to oversee the prosecution. His account intricately weaves together the threads of evidence, particularly focusing on the correspondence found in the trunk of the deceased, Sarah Maria Cornell. The meticulous comparison of letter paper textures and torn edges provides a riveting backdrop for the unfolding narrative.

Jeremiah Hambley, a resident near the old meeting house in Fall River, adds a crucial piece to the puzzle, recalling a tall man accompanied by a woman turning towards the bridge on December 20th. The narrative unfolds further with Iram Smith's storekeeper testimony, detailing Avery's visit on December 8th, setting the stage for the unfolding drama.

As additional witnesses, such as stage driver Stephen Bartlett and steamboat engineer John Orswell, enter the fray, the intricate web of evidence becomes denser. The prosecution masterfully introduces letters, each a potential piece of the puzzle, leading to heated debates and objections from the defense.

The chapter culminates with the attorney general declaring the government's case closed, signaling a pivotal moment in the trial. This chapter promises a riveting exploration of the evidence presented in court, setting the stage for the impending showdown between the prosecution and the defense as they vie for the jury's judgment.

In Chapter 13, the defense takes center stage, launching a spirited counterattack against the prosecution's narrative. Richard K. Randolph, Esq., steps into the legal arena with a fervent opening speech on the ninth day of the trial, challenging the integrity of the prosecution's witnesses and aiming to dismantle the foundation of their case. His strategy is clear: to sow seeds of doubt about the suicide theory and expose what he deems as flawed evidence.

Randolph delves into the intricacies of the knot used in the tragic event, arguing it to be a common one employed by weavers for harness mending—a subtle yet crucial point in challenging the notion of foul play. He scrutinizes the length of the hanging string, dismissing its significance. Mocking the weight given to the paper found in Miss Cornell's bandbox, he positions it as insufficient grounds for suspicion. The medical experts' testimony is discredited as mere theory lacking a factual foundation.

The defense unfolds a comprehensive narrative, delving into Miss Cornell's history, character, and alleged threats of suicide, attempting to paint a portrait of her as a troubled and possibly insane woman. A legion of medical witnesses, some from distant cities, is summoned to challenge the prosecution's medical experts. Their unanimous stance asserts that the fetus was older and the bruises a result of decay, reinforcing the defense's narrative.

As the defense explores the intricate layers of Miss Cornell's life, a multitude of witnesses is paraded, each testifying to her alleged insanity and a history of suicide attempts. The defense strategically challenges key moments, including the Thompson camp meeting, attempting to distance Mr. Avery from Miss Cornell during critical times.

The courtroom drama escalates with a barrage of witnesses challenging the credibility of the prosecution's key players. A striking shift occurs as the defense presents a united front of Methodist witnesses, emphasizing Avery's saintly character and dismissing Miss Cornell as deranged and morally corrupt.

This chapter unfolds as a saga of conflicting testimonies, as the defense deploys a diverse array of tactics to cast doubt on the prosecution's case. The courtroom becomes a battleground of narratives, with the defense orchestrating a meticulous strategy to save Mr. Avery from the looming specter of justice.

In Chapter 14, the climactic moment of the trial arrives as Chief Justice Eddy addresses the jury after the attorney general's closing remarks. The courtroom, filled with an air of anticipation, experiences a profound silence before the venerable chief justice imparts his guidance to the jury. Chief Justice Eddy navigates the complexities of the trial, clarifying the purpose of the evidence presented, especially emphasizing the limited scope of the paper in pencil marks and the evolving admission status of the white letter. He urges the jury to exercise sound discretion, basing their conclusions on common sense and consistency in the circumstantial evidence presented.

The chief justice's charge culminates with a reminder to consider the possibility of suicide as the cause of death, urging the jurors to proceed with coolness, caution, candor, and deliberation. The weight of their responsibility is emphasized, with a reminder that any reasonable doubt should work in favor of the accused.

Following Chief Justice Eddy's address, Mr. Sergeant Tripp takes the stand, and the jury is committed to his charge. The courtroom remains in session until 7 p.m., and as the crowd anxiously watches the courthouse, the church bells toll on a sunshiny Sabbath morning. The tension reaches its peak as the jury, after a night of scrutiny and deliberation, finally delivers its verdict.

The foreman rises to declare, "Not guilty," sending shockwaves through the courtroom. The assembly erupts into a tumultuous response, revealing the deep-seated emotions surrounding the case. Despite the chaos, the clerk records the verdict, and Ephraim K. Avery is declared not guilty. The acquitted man, surrounded by his supporters, leaves the courtroom, marked by the vindictive glares of those who sought justice for Sarah Cornell.

The conclusion of this chapter reflects on Avery's post-acquittal life, revealing that he chose to leave the neighborhood for safety.

Rumors circulate about his whereabouts, and it is disclosed that he eventually moved west to Ohio, leading a peaceful life as a farmer until his death. The narrative closes with a poignant acknowledgment of Avery's acts of charity and a reflection on the enduring legacy of Sarah Cornell's tragic tale among the factory folk of Fall River. The trial may have ended, but the echoes of the events continue to resonate through the collective memory of the community.

In Chapter 15, the narrative takes a chilling turn as I delve into the haunting tale of Sarah Maria Cornell's tragic demise. Prompted by a dream about Blas Trujillos and inspired by a list of murder victims, I embarked on a journey to give voice to Sarah whose story has been long forgotten or overlooked.

After inviting the spirit of Sarah Maria Cornell to share her story, my visions unfolded like a modern-day motion picture. The chapter opens with Sarah's introduction as an innocent and devout woman, standing amidst a crowd at an old-fashioned camp-style church gathering. Dressed in a simple brown ensemble, she captures the attention of the charismatic Reverend Ephraim K. Avery.

The narrative takes a dramatic turn as Reverend Avery, fixated on Sarah, orchestrates a meeting behind the meeting house, revealing his ulterior motives. Through vivid visions, the storyteller paints a picture of seduction and betrayal, depicting their clandestine encounters in the woods and a nearby hotel.

As the story progresses, the storyteller unveils the unfolding tragedy of Sarah's life. Sarah, genuinely devoted to her religious beliefs, is manipulated by Avery's false promises and deceit. The vision intensifies as Sarah discovers she is pregnant, and Avery reneges on his vows, proposing a sinister plan to eliminate the unborn child.

The atmosphere becomes increasingly sinister as Avery coerces Sarah into taking an abortifacient, leading to a horrifying scene of assault and manipulation. The storyteller vividly describes the chilling moment Avery strangles Sarah, staging her death to appear as a suicide. The visuals, hauntingly detailed, capture the brutality of the crime, leaving a lasting impression on the reader.

As Sarah's lifeless body is staged in a haystack, the storyteller skillfully conveys the desolation of the crime scene. The chapter concludes with reflections on the vision, emphasizing the heinous nature of Avery's actions. Sarah, now in heaven, is portrayed as forgiving, viewing her murderer as a pitiable victim of evil.

This final chapter immerses the reader in a tale of manipulation, betrayal, and violence, shedding light on the Terrible Haystack Murder that shook the community in 1832. The narrative skillfully weaves together elements of suspense, horror, and tragedy, leaving the audience with a profound sense of the darkness that can reside within the human soul.

Together, Sarah and I navigate the spectral labyrinth of history, shedding light on long-forgotten secrets. Sarah Cornell's story serves as a powerful reminder that even the darkest of secrets cannot remain hidden forever, and, in the end, the truth will always be revealed.

PRELIMINARY CASE FILE

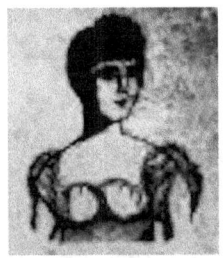

Sarah Maria Cornell

Case Summary

Name of Deceased: Sarah Maria Cornell

Date of Birth: est. May 3, 1803

Date of Death: December 20, 1832

Location: Tiverton, Rhode Island

Deceased Found by: Farmer John Durfee

Relationship to the Deceased: None

Complainant: John Durfee

Relationship to the Deceased: None

Witnesses: No eye-witnesses to the murder

Estimated Time of Death: The evening of December 20, 1832

Positions of Body: Sarah was found hanging from a cord tied to the roof of a haystack.

Wounds: Rope burn to throat; bruising on abdomen and thighs

Blood Splatters: N/A

Autopsy Findings: Dr. Wilbur initially declared her death a suicide —that she had killed herself in despair because the father of her unborn child was a married minister.

Reported Cause of Death: Choking by the hands or by hanging.

Disposition: Cold Case—the jury decided there was not enough evidence to convict Ephraim Avery of murder.

Informant Sources (Adapted From the following Books):

Author Unknown. (1833). *The Terrible Hay-Stack Murder: The Awful Life and Curious Trial of the Rev. Ephraim K. Avery.* Barclay & Co. Publishers.

Author Unknown. (1833). *Report of the Trial of the Rev. Ephraim K. Avery, Methodist Minster, for the Murder of Sarah Maria Cornell at Tiverton.* William Stodart Publishing.

Was it Suicide?

On Friday morning, December 21, 1832, John Durfee, a farmer residing in the little village of Tiverton, Rhode Island, about half a mile from the bridge at Fall River, was passing through a lot near his house with a team of his farm hands. Within a few rods (approximately 17 yards) of a little circular enclosure containing a stack of hay, he observed the body of a beautiful girl hanging in the yard on a stake set up against the stack. Horrified at the sight, he jumped from his wagon and cautiously approached. The head of the girl was thrown forward with her face turned toward him. Her long, dark hair shrouded her face like a veil. He gently pushed aside the raven tresses of her hair which revealed the pale, cold face of a dead woman. She wore a long cloak that was hooked together the whole length up and down, except for one hook over the breast. Her hood was on; her shoes were off; her feet were close together, and her legs were carried back so that her knees came within a few inches of the ground, and under them, her clothes were smoothly folded. The cord from which she was hung was a small marline twine (a light, two-stranded rope) doubled around her neck and fastened to a stake about six inches from the top. The top of her head was a few inches below the top of the stake, against which her right cheek rested.

From her dress and general appearance, Durfee judged the dead girl to be a factory worker, and with an involuntary shudder, he thought:

"Poor girl! Sick and tired of a life of toil, she has sought to obtain rest by destroying herself."

He turned away from the sad sight and called loudly to several of his farm hands who were in sight.

"Hey! Come here! Some poor girl has hung herself in the stackyard. She's dead."

At this command, three men came toward him, and one, with more presence of mind than his companions, quickened his pace to a run and cried:

"She may still be alive. Cut her down."

Durfee quickly leaped the fence and attempted to lift the body to slip the cord over the top of the stake, but her weight was too much for him, so he turned to his companions and called for a knife. One of the three men standing by handed him a small knife, and severing the cord, he lowered the rigid body gently to the ground. "I was right," said Durfee sadly. "She's dead!"

After several minutes of silence, one of the men discovered the dead woman's little shoes, a short distance from the body. He picked them up, and after holding them for a minute or so, placed them closer to the body. A large red bandana handkerchief, such as was usually carried by men in those days, was discovered lying on the ground on the other side of the body.

"What will we do with her?" Asked Durfee, motioning toward the body and turning to his companions.

"Just bury her!" replied the old, rugged-looking man of the party. "She is dead, poor thing, and we can't do her any good."

"Shouldn't we go for the coroner?" Asked the youngest man among them.

"Yes, we should get the coroner," replied Durfee.

"Who wants to go?" asked the young man.

The old man cried out, "Durfee should go. It's his land! Mr. Durfee, we'll stay with the body while you go for the coroner."

Durfee started toward the village, and the other men left standing by the body turned to each other and began discussing the sad occurrence.

"Who is she?" asked the old man. "Does anybody know her?"

They all shook their heads at this query, and one of the middle-aged men speculated:

"I guess she must be a weaver because she's got a weaver's knot around the stake." He stepped forward to the stake and lifted the twine. No bigger than a goose quill, it was double-looped around the stake with four ends hanging down. After analyzing the knot, which occupied him for a minute or so, he replied:

"She is more a sailor than a weaver, there are a few half-hitches around the standing part" (meaning, the part that led to her neck).

At this, the others examined the cord and knot, and the one who had made the observation walked a short distance away towards his work for the day. The ground was rough and uneven, strewn with stones, and overgrown with bushes and briars. The dead woman had worn a piece of comb in her hair. The man found it on the ground twenty rods (about 110 yards) away from where they had discovered her body. It was on a path that the cattle had made by walking back and forth between the haystack and the pasture. He carried it back to the party still grouped around the stack, and one of the men asked:

"Ain't the cord she was hung with like the twine used to make those bags Durfee got from the calico works for us to sit on while we're drilling?"

"I don't know, but I'll see," said the man, and cutting off a small piece of the twine around the stake, he walked away with it in his hand to a wagon about one hundred rods (550 yards) from the stack, in which were kept a lot of gunny bags and tools used in drilling rock. The bags had been used as casings for cotton cloths and were sewn with twine. He compared this twine with the piece of cord in his hand, and there was no perceptible difference in size or color.

After making the comparison, he said, "Here is where it came from. She could get a piece long enough if she unraveled the whole bag."

By this time the coroner had arrived, and with him a motley crew of men, women, and children, morbidly curious to gaze, gape, and stare at the dead woman before them.

"Why, it's Maria Cornell!" cried a young girl. "She worked with me at the mill in Fall River."

She was interrupted by the coroner, who, having summoned a jury from the crowd, ordered them to read the law governing such cases. The body was then taken up and carried to the house of Durfee, followed by the jury and the crowd. When the house was reached, the body was placed on a bed, and the jury proceeded to take evidence. The girl who had first identified the body informed the coroner that Sarah had boarded with Mrs. Hathaway.

At this point, the coroner directed one of the men present to go to the place mentioned and retrieve the girl's personal belongings; if she had any, and to summon Mrs. Hathaway and the members of her family, as well as the dead girl's friends and work companions.

The inquest began. Farmer Durfee and his companions testified to the finding of the body in the position and after the manner before described, and after their testimonies, the jury adjourned to the stack yard to view the spot. After making themselves thoroughly familiar with the surroundings, they returned to the house. By this time the messenger had returned from Fall River, bringing with him the witnesses, personal belongings of the deceased, and two physicians.

Except for the everyday articles of clothing that made up the young girl's wardrobe, her trunk contained nothing, which would be likely to give a probable clue as to why she would take her life, if, indeed, she had done so; however, in a bandbox in her room, the messenger found one red letter, one yellow letter, and one white letter, all addressed to "Sarah M. Cornell," and one white letter directed to "Rev. Ira Bidwell." The letter directed to Mr. Bidwell was sealed; the rest were open. Near the bottom of the box was a small slip of paper and a piece of pencil. These were handed to the jury.

Harriet Hathaway testified that Sarah Cornell had boarded with her for three weeks. The last time she saw her alive was the previous afternoon. She said that Sarah wanted her dinner earlier than usual because she needed to leave for a meeting before the mill closed. She left just before sunset and said that she was going to Joseph Durfee's and would return before nine o'clock. She seemed a lot more cheerful than usual. I know she was planning on coming back because she left a trunk and bandbox in her room, which I gave to John Durfee this morning to be taken to the coroner. She was not in the habit of being out in the evenings, except when, as she said, she went to class meetings.

According to the testimony of Lucy Hathaway (daughter of the preceding witness), she worked in the same room at the mill where Sarah worked. Lucy said Sarah left the mill the day before, about half past five, and that she had mentioned the scheduled meeting to her a week earlier.

The "loom boss" at the mill corroborated this testimony, and after deliberating a few minutes, the jury adjourned to wait for the results of the post-mortem examination and the investigation of the letters found in the dead girl's room.

So far the general impression seemed to prevail that the girl had committed suicide, but none of her friends and acquaintances could explain why.

~ 3 ~

IT MIGHT BE MURDER!

On Saturday, the coroner's jury assembled again, and the physicians who had conducted the post-mortem examination made a statement to them, as did several other witnesses, but no sworn evidence was taken, so they adjourned until Monday.

Upon their reassembling, Dr. Foster Hooper testified:

I reside in Fall River and have practiced medicine for five years. I have examined the body of S. M. Cornell. The neck was indented horizontally and equally to the depth of three-eighths to half an inch. On the right side of the face, under the ear, there was the appearance of two strands having passed, pinching the skin between them. On the right jaw and the right temple were irregular indentations, as though the face, after the circulation had stopped, had pressed on some hard substance. The skin was not broken. The lungs were engorged with black blood. On the knees were several scratches or slight wounds that drew blood; likewise, stains, as of dirt, and green spots, as of the juice of grass. There were a few scratches on the left leg below the knee, and the skin was rubbed off in two places the size of fourpence. On the inner knee, a mark of dirt extended up toward the thigh. The right side of the abdomen was of a livid hue, which appeared to me to be caused by incipient putrefaction. On the left side, above the hip, there was a considerable

> contusion. *The uterus contained a female fetus about half-grown. It required a rather minute examination to ascertain the sex. The features were not very distorted. The tongue was caught between the teeth. The face was pale.*

Dr. Thomas Wilbur, the other physician, confirmed the above. When the two doctors had finished their testimony, a shudder ran through the throng crowded into the inquest room, and murmurs of "It was murder, not suicide!" were heard. Silencing the tumult, the coroner read to the jury these words from the slip of paper found in the bottom of the bandbox at Miss Cornell's boarding house:

December 20th.

If I am missing, inquire of Rev. Ephraim Avery of Bristol. He will know where I am.

S. M. Cornell

The murmur of surprise in the crowd changed to hoarse cries of indignation as the coroner finished reading, and one man shouted,

"It's the person who did it. He's the father of her child, and he murdered her to save himself from exposure."

Another voice cried, "If that's so, perhaps he wrote her the letters. Read the letters."

The coroner picked up the red letter and read it as follows:

> *Providence, RI*
>
> *November, 1831." Dear Sister:*
>
> *I received your letter and should have answered it before now, but I thought I would wait until this opportunity. As I told you, I am*

willing to help you and do things for you. As circumstances are, I would rather you come to this place, viz., Bristol, on the 18th, of December, stop at the hotel, stay until six in the evening, and then go directly up the main street to the brick building near the stone meeting house, where I will meet you and talk with you. When you stop at the tavern, either inquire for work or go out to the street in the pretense of looking for someone else, and I may see you. Say nothing about me or my family. Should it storm on the 18th, come on the 20th. If you cannot come and it will be more convenient to meet me at the Methodist meeting house in Summerset, just over the ferry, on either of the above evenings, I will meet you there at the same time. Or, if you cannot do either, I will come to Fall River on one of the above evenings, back of the same meeting house where I first saw you, at any hour you say on either of the above evenings, when there will be the least passing traffic. Sometime before the mills stop work. I will come if it does not storm very hard. If it storms on the first date, I'll come on the second one. Write to me soon and tell me which. When you write, remember to direct your letters to Betsey Hills, Bristol, and not to me. I am afraid your last letter was broken open. Wear your calash and not your plain bonnet. (A calash is a type of collapsible bonnet made to accommodate large hairstyles, and was popular from the mid-18th century well into the 19th century.) You can send your letter by mail from: Yours, etc., "S. M. C. B. H." Let me still enjoy the secret. Keep the letters in your bosom, or burn them up.

The letter was addressed on the envelope: Miss Sarah M. Cornell, Fall River, Mass. To be left at Mrs. Cole's. The crowd remained silent, and the jury looked very grave. Taking up the white letter, the coroner read:

Fall River, December the 8th.
I will be there on the 20th, if the weather is pleasant, at the place

named at six o'clock; if not pleasant, the next Monday evening. Say nothing.

This missive was directed to *Miss Sarah M. Cornell, Fall River*, and laying it down, the coroner opened and read the yellow letter as follows:

November the 13th, 1832

I have just received your letter with no small surprise and I will do all you ask, only keep your secret. I want you to write me as soon as you get this, naming some time and place where I can see you, then look for an answer before I come, and I will say whether it is convenient or not regarding the time. I will keep your letters until I see you, and I wish you to keep mine and have them there at the time. Write soon. Say nothing to anyone. Yours in haste.

This letter was directed to Miss Sarah M. Cornell, Fall River, Mass., and was postmarked to Warren, RI, on Nov. 14. The coroner's jury of Friday and Saturday had partly agreed upon a verdict of death by suicide, but these new developments changed the ultimate verdict to this::

We find that the said S. M. Cornell came to her death by hanging or choking at the hands of some person or persons to this jury unknown. And we also find that suspicion points to Rev. E. K. Avery, of Bristol, and we recommend that he be apprehended and held for examination.

The body of the dead girl was left in the hands of her friends. They washed it tenderly and combed and arranged the long hair that had been her pride. The scene of the murder became an object of great curiosity, and thousands flocked to the spot, eager to get a glimpse of the dead girl's face. The coroner had ordered the body to be buried, and when, late on Monday afternoon, the coffin was carried to the grave, such a concourse of people followed it as had never been seen before.

The theory of murder was believed in by all, and expressions of indignation against the priestly man who had been accused of the crime were strong and general. Business was almost entirely suspended in Fall River, so great was the excitement, and little else was talked of but the murdered girl and her suspected murderer.

~ 4 ~

THE VIGILANCE COMMITTEE

Sunday is usually a peaceful day among the Puritanical New Englanders, but the Sunday that followed the murder of Sarah Maria Cornell was an exception. It was known in Fall River that the paper and letters given in the last chapter had been found, and even if the coroner's jury, which was newly appointed to take up the investigation on the next day, returned a verdict of suicide, public opinion, which is in this country a most powerful and widely felt influence, declared that Sarah Cornell was murdered—foully murdered—and her blood cried out for vengeance against her murderer.

From the surrounding country, men, women, and children flocked to the center of attraction, and even from distant states came dire threats against the life and peace of the suspected murderer, who up to this time had been a preacher of the gospel, connected, and in high standing, with a most numerous and respectable denomination of Christians. A denomination that at that time, in this country, numbered ten thousand licensed preachers; six hundred thousand members; and three million hearers. The Methodist Church probably never before had so zealous and eloquent an advocate as the Rev. Ephraim K. Avery, and his fame extended over the length and breadth of the country. His services were always in demand, and thousands had been converted to the Methodist faith through his efforts. Like a celebrated preacher of more extended fame and more recent notoriety, he had enshrined himself in the hearts of his hearers—an idol—that no suspicion, however strong, no evidence, however conclusive, no imputation, however well grounded, could displace. Holding the position that he did, is it any wonder that all evidence impugning the character of their beloved pastor was at first ridiculed and hooted as beyond reason, and then as the chain of circumstances connecting him closely with the deed grew stronger and stronger, it was openly assailed and resisted by these people? On the other hand, a strong feeling also existed among those who might be called anti-religious, who thought that they might throw insults at religion itself by procuring the conviction of the accused murderer. To this cause of excitement may be added the natural jealousy felt by other sects of that to which Ephraim belonged, and a still additional cause of excitement may be found in the situation of the deceased. She was a factory girl from the village of Fall River, in the state of Rhode Island. Her working-class status strengthened public interest and amplified the public sentiment regarding her murder across all of New England. People living in the vicinity of the scene of the murder, when the evidence implicating Ephraim Avery began to gather, recalled having seen a man who fit his description lurking about on the day that preceded the evening of her murder. The man who had found the body, Durfee, accompanied by a citizen of Fall River, Seth Darling, went to Bristol on Sunday to have Ephraim taken in by the authorities. They applied to a magistrate, but for some reason, he took no action in the matter.

On Monday, while the newly empaneled coroner's jury was still in consultation, a mass meeting of the citizens of Fall River was held, and a Committee of Vigilance, consisting of thirteen members selected from among the best of her citizens, was appointed to ascertain facts relative to the murder of the girl, Sarah Maria Cornell. A committee of five was also chosen to assist in the prosecution.

Twenty or thirty prominent men in Fall River pledged themselves to bear the expenses of the investigation.

As the days passed excitement reached a near fever pitch, and on Christmas Day, a large body of the inhabitants of Fall River went over to Bristol and demanded the surrender of the hypocritical murderer. They surrounded his house, and several times his life was in danger. Evidence against him was quickly accumulating.

The postmaster at Bristol testified that Ephraim was in the habit of receiving letters from Fall River and that no letters had ever passed through the office addressed to Betsey Hills, and indeed, no such person was known or had ever been heard of. John Orswell, the engineer of the boat King Philip, running from Providence to Fall River, said that he recognized the red letter found in Sarah Cornell's trunk as one given to him at Providence to deliver by a man who fit the description of Ephraim. Deputy Sheriff Paul, of Fall River, escorted Orswell to the house of the preacher to see if he could positively identify him as the man. Upon reaching the house, they found it surrounded by a mob of angry people. Forcing their way through the crowd, they created an entrance to the house. Upstairs, they found several gentlemen sitting around a small room. The deputy sheriff asked Orswell if he could identify either one of those present as the man who gave him the letter.

"No, sir," replied Orswell, scanning the faces of the gentlemen before him. "If either one of these gentlemen is Mr. Avery, he did not give me the letter."

Mr. Paul shouted for Ephraim Avery to come out of hiding, and as he came in from another room, Orwell stared at him intently and said:

"That is the man who gave me the letter!"

There was a murmur of surprise at this bold accusation, but with a brazen air of arrogance, the preacher faced him and inquired:

"How was the man who gave you this letter dressed?"

Orswell replied, "I did not notice his dress particularly, only that he wore a cloak and a black hat."

"Will you be willing to go before a court and swear that I am the man?"

"I have not said that I would," replied Orswell.

"Ah, you see," said Ephraim triumphantly turning to the others in the room. "He cannot swear positively that I am the man." And then, turning to Orswell, he said, "It would be gratifying to me and my friends to know what you think about my being the man."

"According to the best of my judgment and recollection, you are the man."

"Did the man have glasses?"

"No!"

Again, a look of triumph passed over Avery's face, and turning to the party in the room, he said, "Did any of you ever know me to go outdoors without my glasses?"

"No!" they answered in one breath. "Never!"

Avery then adjusted his spectacles and, turning to Orswell, said, "Do I look like the man now?"

"It does not alter your features, in my view, one bit," replied Orswell firmly."

While this examination was in progress, the crowd in the street below grew impatient, and several of the more resolute individuals gained entrance to the house. At the request of the deputy sheriff, however, they left and the examination continued to proceed quietly. It was finally decided to take Avery before the trial court, and it was accordingly done. The justice commanded his detention, and surety for his appearance being given, he was held in custody at his own house until a warrant was legally obtained for his arrest, upon which Judge Randall took his recognizance, with sureties for $20,000, for his appearance at the March term of the Supreme Court. Much indignation was felt in Fall River when it was learned that he had been allowed to escape under bail. Public sentiment demanded that he be incarcerated in the common jail, like other suspected malefactors, and a movement was made to obtain a new examination.

At the request of many of the prominent citizens of Fall River, the body of the murdered girl was exhumed, and Doctors Hooper and Wilbur submitted the body to a more rigorous examination. The result, when it was made known to the public, increased their rage against Avery, for it was found that an abortion had been attempted, and experts theorized that the girl had met Ephraim at the stack yard by appointment and that he had attempted to abort the fetus. The pain of the operation had caused her to lose consciousness, and while in this state, Avery had placed the cord around her neck, and after strangling her, he hung the body over the haystack.

Several parties, living in the vicinity of the stack yard, heard screams and cries of pain or terror on the night of the murder, and at about the hour when it was supposed the crime was committed, there was positive evidence tracing Avery to the island on that evening. Circumstances were quickly hedging in on him, and he would surely need a miracle to escape the punishment that his heinous crime deserved.

~ 5 ~

EPHRAIM WINS HER AFFECTION
AND BETRAYS HER HONOR

Sarah Maria Cornell was born May 3, 1803, in the little town of Rupert, Vermont. She had one sister, who married Grindall Rawson. From an early age, Sarah, or, as she was more familiarly called, Sally, was noted for her piety, truth, and religious enthusiasm. She was very devoted and, at an early age, connected herself with the Methodist church. Sally was noted for her beauty, which was of that ruddy pink and white type peculiar to the girls of the Green Mountain State, and had many admirers, but somehow she was never suited. She preserved her beauty despite Father Time, and at thirty, she passed very readily for a girl of twenty. Her father being a poor man, she early entered a cotton factory at Dover, New Hampshire, and worked subsequently in many of the principal mills in New England. In every town where she resided, she was distinguished for her religious zeal. She attended church regularly every Sunday and frequently spent several evenings during the week at class or prayer meetings.

Miss Cornell met Ephraim Avery about five years before her murder and regarded him as a sort of demi-god. She listened in rapture to his teachings and looked up to him as the embodiment of all that was good and pure. Until August, before her death, the relations between the two had been marked by no special event other than the ordinary friendly companionship of pastor and parishioner. In May 1832, she came to Woodstock, Connecticut, and sought and obtained work in the factory there. She connected herself with the Methodist church, presenting as her credentials a letter from her late pastor in Lowell, Massachusetts.

In August of that year, the Methodists held a great camp meeting and revival at Thompson, near Providence, Rhode Island, which Sarah attended. Rev. Avery was also in attendance and took a leading part in the religious exercises.

When Miss Cornell reached the grounds, Ephraim was in the act of delivering one of his impassioned discourses, and in rapt wonder, she stood listening to the burning words as they fell from the lips of the man she admired so blindly. Tears filled her eyes, and she was so affected by the sermon that she was obliged to turn away and recover her wonted tranquility of mind in the seclusion of the deep forest. When she was a little more composed, she turned to retrace her steps and, on her way, met the object of her thoughts coming toward her. As he approached, a blush of pleasure suffused her face; her eyes drooped, and when he halted in front of her and extended his hand, she raised her eyes timidly to his face and held out her little hand, which was seized and pressed with evident warmth by the minister.

"And how are you, my dear sister?" He asked, retaining her hand.

"Oh! I am very well, sir," she replied.

"I am very glad to see you," he said, bending nearer until his warm breath fanned her cheek. '

"Thank you," replied Sarah, modestly stepping back a pace and withdrawing her hand.

"I still have your letter," he said.

"Indeed, you promised to destroy it when I saw you a year ago in Lowell. It is of no great consequence whether you retain it or destroy it. Nevertheless, I don't want anyone else to get hold of it. I was penitent when I wrote it and knew that I had done wrong in talking so much about one of the sisters of the church. But you promised me if I wrote a letter acknowledging my fault, you would read it to Sister Coulson, and I would be forgiven.

Well, I read it to her, and she forgave you. I indeed promised to destroy the letter, but the temptation to retain some memento of one who held, and does to this day hold, so high a place in my regard as you do, was too great, and I have treasured it ever since."

"It is very gratifying to know that my friends think so well of me," replied Sarah.

"I do think a great deal of you," said the minister, with emphasis, "and I want to talk with you some time where we will not be interrupted."

"Well, sir!"

"If you like, I will meet you tonight at the house when the horn blows for preaching."

"You can come if you wish," she said. "Goodbye!" and she passed by him and went toward the preacher's stand.

"Good-bye! I will be punctual," said the preacher.

That night, when the signal was given for the services to begin, Sarah was standing outside the door. Avery came toward her and, after looking into the tent, said:

"There is no room in the tent for us. It is full. We can't have any talk there—go into the woods, and I will join you."

As directed, Sarah walked down the road, away from the tents, and Avery turned back, apparently toward the ground, but after she had passed on a little way, he came from another direction and met her. Taking his arm, the two passed on into the woods. After going some distance, they came to a smooth, grassy plot of ground, and, motioning toward the foot of a giant tree, whose gnarled roots twisted themselves into a natural couch, Avery asked her to sit down. She did so, and he placed himself beside her.

After a moment's silence, Avery drew nearer and passed his arm around her waist. He was trembling violently, and his voice was husky.

"I want to ask you a question, Sarah," he said at length.

She made no reply, and he went on.

"You must know that I have a very high regard for you—that I love you," and with this confession, he bent over and, drawing her face closer, kissed her hotly.

"Sir! Mr. Avery!" cried the startled girl, struggling to break away from him. "Remember you are a married man, and I am a virtuous woman."

"As God is my judge!" said Avery fiercely, "I love you—madly—devotedly—better than all else—and a wife—no!—not even she shall stand between us."

In vain, the frightened girl endeavored to release herself. His strong arms held her fast. He drew her head down on his bosom and rained kiss after kiss upon her lips and cheeks. His breath came hot and fast, and he pressed her convulsively to his heart. With a last effort, she endeavored to struggle to her feet, but still, he held her fast. Her senses seemed deadened in a mystic spell. She closed her eyes; her tense muscles relaxed, and she burst into tears.

The tempter's artifices had proved successful, and the prey was his. Several hours elapsed before the pair returned to the campgrounds. He was ahead, elated over his easy victory, yet frightened when cool reflection taught him the awfulness of such a crime, committed by a minister of God, and she, a poor, weak woman, degraded in her own eyes and, with a sinking heart, like a meek lamb going to the slaughter, followed in the footsteps of the man who was henceforth to be her master.

~ 6 ~

SARAH IS GOING TO BE A
MOTHER

At the time of the camp meeting, Sarah was living with her brother-in-law, Grindall Rawson, assisting him in the management of his tailor shop—she had remained at the factory for a short time. While she resided at his house, it was noticed that she seemed to be subject to unusual fits of melancholy. At times she would be found in tears, and when questioned as to the cause of her agitation, she would exhibit much confusion, reply evasively, and if pressed, turn the matter off with a laugh that, to the ears of her wondering friends, sounded strangely hollow and unnatural.

In October, Miss Cornell declared her intention of leaving Woodstock to work in the mills at Fall River. Her brother-in-law, Mr. Rawson, endeavored to dissuade her, and when he assured her that she could make his house her home so long as she chose to remain there, she burst into tears and, between her sobs, gave utterance to these words:

"If you knew all, you would not say so. 1 am undone—undone—and I dare no longer raise my head in respectable society."

"What do you mean, Sarah?" inquired Rawson, kindly.

"Oh, dear," she cried, "I dare not tell!"

"Dare not tell!" echoed Rawson.

"It was not my fault," she continued. "I could not resist him."

"Him! Who?"

"Mr. Avery."

"What has he done to you?"

She lowered her head and again burst into tears. Finding it impossible to gain any intelligence from her, Rawson left the room and sent in her sister, his wife. To her, Miss Cornell confessed her shame and expressed the belief that she would, in a few months, become a mother.

Startled somewhat by this intelligence, Mrs. Rawson called her husband, and in his presence, Sarah reiterated her previous statement. After talking the matter over, it was finally agreed that, as Miss Cornell was not positive as to her exact condition, she had better go to Fall River, and when it was certain she was in a delicate situation, inform Mr. Avery of the fact.

Accordingly, Miss Cornell came to Fall River and, readily obtaining employment, secured board at the house of Elijah Cole. It was while she was here that she received the red letter from the hands of Orswell, who was positive that it was handed to him for delivery by Avery. She lived very privately while here and at times appeared lost in thought; again, she would appear animated and gay, but it was forced.

By reference to the letter, it will be seen that Avery made an appointment with Miss Cornell on the 20th of October. The night in question was one of those beautiful evenings so peculiarly a feature of the New England Indian Summer. The stars shone out in all their brilliance, and the light emitted from so many countless worlds was nearly as strong as that white luster reflected from the moon. It was Saturday, and the great mills, which gave employment to so many busy hands, were dark and deserted; only the streets presented a lively appearance, filled as they were with gay throngs of the operatives, male and female, unusually merry in the knowledge that there was no work on the morrow.

The Methodists had been holding a revival service that lasted four days, and after supper, Miss Cornell donned her shawl and hood and told her friends, the Coles, that she was "going to meeting"—in reality, to meet the man who had betrayed her honor.

She walked through the streets quickly and, with an averted head, endeavored as much as possible to shun observation. Several of her acquaintances met her and spoke, but she passed on without heeding them. She was nearly in front of the old meeting house on Main Street when a tall man, wearing a long cloak, his face shrouded by a broad-brimmed hat, came toward her. Taking his arm, the two retraced their steps and shortly turned into Spring Street. Neither spoke until, in the course of their walk, they passed the outskirts of the town. When they were entirely alone and the lights from the nearest house shone dimly, Miss Cornell halted and, facing her companion, said:

"Well!"

"I came, Sarah," replied Ephraim, "to see if this matter can be settled."

"How do you propose to settle it? Can you give me back my virtue and my good name?"

"No!—That is—really—you are sarcastic—you are too severe, Sarah."

"Too foolish, perhaps, would be better," was the disdainful reply.

"Well! You do act foolishly when you talk about being ruined and all that, just because you happen to be in an unfortunate situation that a few months of retirement among strangers will make all right. No one that you need care about will know of it, and as to the child, it can be easily disposed of."

"My sister suspects my condition."

"Nonsense! How could she, unless you have been foolish enough to tell her?"

"Foolish or not, I have told her, and I will tell others. I will tell the world! I will brand you the wicked hypocrite you are! It will ruin me, but I will have the satisfaction of knowing that I will drag your good name down with mine, in shame and ignominy!"

A hot flush mantled her cheek while she spoke, and her eyes blazed with a ballistic fire. She peered intently at her companion's face to see what effect her words had on him. Instead of dropping to his knees and asking for forgiveness, the villain threw back his head and burst into a loud laugh.

"Ha! Ha! Ha!" he shouted. "I believe that you are demented. Who do you suppose would believe the story if you were foolish enough to tell it?"

"But it is the truth!"

"Granted! But I will deny it. I am a man of good standing in the community, a minister of the gospel, revered, and respected. You are a poor factory girl, and like the majority of your class, you have a doubtful reputation. Which do you think the world will believe?"

The question had not presented itself to her in this light before, and conscious that even now he had the advantage over her, she dropped her head and burst into tears. Ephraim stood regarding her for several minutes without speaking, and then, laying his hand on her shoulder, said, "There, there! Sarah. Dry your eyes, and listen to reason."

Her sobs continued; he passed his arm around her waist and drew her toward him.

"If you will listen to me, it will be all right," he said, stroking her face. "Come, let us walk back toward town. I must not be away long."

Without a word, she allowed him to draw her arm into his, and thus together they retraced their steps. He assured her that he meant to stand by her and help her and that if she would only retire into the country where she was not known until after her confinement, it would be all right. She could come back, and no one would be wiser for it. During the progress of the conversation, they entered town, near the spot where she had met him. She had just given her consent to his plan when a man and woman passed them. Sarah looked up and recognized the couple as Bailey Borden and his wife. Mrs. Borden nodded, and she was on the point of returning the greeting but was restrained by Avery, who, when anyone approached, averted his face.

"Don't acknowledge anyone while I am with you," said Ephraim impatiently. "You don't know what might occur, and I should keep silent on this matter."

Sarah promised, and Ephraim shortly bade her goodnight. The two separated, she to return to her lodging to spend the night in tears and anguish, and he to mingle with the church people.

~ 7 ~

THE FATAL DAY

It was about three weeks before her death that Miss Cornell left the Coles and went to board with Mrs. Harriet Hathaway. Her landlady's daughter worked by her side in the mill, and the two became quite intimate.

One day, a short time after she took up residence with the Hathaways, she showed her friend a white letter, which she said she had received that day. It contained only a few lines and was the one from Avery making the appointment for the evening of the 20th of December.

It was the afternoon of the fatal day, and Miss Cornell was working at her loom when one of the girls in the room approached and asked, "Sarah, can you let me have two shillings until payday? I need an apron very much, and I don't have the money to buy one."

"Certainly," replied Miss Cornell, taking out her pocketbook, "and I will give you the money to buy one for me, too." Then, turning to Miss Hathaway, she said, "Don't you want one, Lucy?"

The girl replied in the negative, and after handing the money for tin aprons to the young lady, she said, "On second thought, you had better get me the stuff, and I will make one for myself. If you and Lucy will help me get my web (probably a first industrial-age type of sewing machine) out, I can easily make it while the loom is fixing."

The two girls promised to assist her, and after the girl who had borrowed the money went back to her work, Miss Cornell seemed very distracted. Her friend rallied her on her melancholy, and she replied, "I don't feel very well, Lucy."

"Are you sick? What is the matter?"

"I have been unwell ever since the camp meeting at Thompson. It originated there."

"What seems to be the matter?"

Miss Cornell blushed at this question and, after a moment's hesitation, approached her friend, and they held a whispered conversation for several minutes. Finally, Miss Hathaway spoke aloud:

"But you say it originated at the camp meeting."

"Yes, and I will never go to one again. I saw things at Thompson that disgusted me, between a church member and a minister, and that minister was a married man, too."

Her friend thought a little strangely of this somewhat ambiguous accusation but said nothing, and just before five o'clock, Sarah left the mill and went directly to her boarding house.

"You are home early, Sarah," said Mrs. Hathaway as she entered.

"Yes, Ma'am, I am going to Joseph Durfee's, but I will be back soon, I think, before nine o'clock anyway."

"Do you want your supper?"

"Just a cup of tea and a biscuit. I am not very hungry."

Mrs. Hathaway bustled about to prepare the supper, and Sarah, trilling a favorite song, went upstairs to dress. These humble preparations for her journey were soon completed, and she was in the act of leaving the room when she stopped and, taking a piece of paper from her writing desk, hastily scribbled a few lines thereon, and folding up the slip, placed it with the pencil in the bottom of her bandbox.

There, she said to herself, *if he wants me to go away tonight and Mrs. Hathaway should get alarmed on account of my absence, that will give her a clue. If I come back tonight, I can destroy it.*

While she was eating her supper, she seemed unusually merry and lighthearted, for she was thinking of the deliverance from shame near at hand and chatted away with Mrs. Hathaway as she had never done before. When the meal was finished, she kissed the landlady goodbye and started in the direction of Tiverton. The mills were not yet closed, and it being an unusually cold night, she met but a few people, and these were too busy trying to keep warm to pay any particular attention to her.

Just before she reached the bridge, Avery came toward her from a spot where he had been watching in the rear of the old meeting house, which had been the place of assignment for all their meetings.

He had a parcel in his hand wrapped in a red handkerchief, and with a simple word of greeting, Sarah took his arm, and the two walked along the road to Tiverton. It was now quite dark, and as they trudged along, Miss Cornell asked: "Where are we going?"

"To Durfee's farm. As I came along this afternoon, I noticed he had a large stack of hay right next to the road. We can sit down in the shelter of that and be as comfortable as though we were in a house."

"Have you come to any conclusion as to what should be done?" she asked.

"Yes!"

"Well, where shall I go? Have you found a place where no one would be likely to find it?"

"You need not go away at all."

"But if I stay, I shall be disgraced."

"No! I will fix that."

"How, pray tell?"

"Wait until we get to the haystack, and I will tell you."

She said nothing more after this but drew her cloak around her and clung closer to the arm of her companion.

Avoiding Durfee's house, they reached the haystack and seated themselves on the sheltered side.

"Now," she said, " what is your plan?"

Avery made no reply to this direct question for several minutes, and then in a low voice urged her to consent to a nefarious scheme, which he had concocted and perfected in all its details with the cool, devilish precision of a Rulof. He used every argument that words could compass, and at last, controlled by the same mysterious influence that had wrought her ruin, Miss Cornell consented to his plan.

Suddenly the quiet of that lonely spot was disturbed by shrill screams of mingled terror and pain, and the helpless girl, crying, "God have mercy! You have killed me!." Then, she fell backward into a dead swoon.

Avery started to his feet with guilty fear, and stared wildly about him! But no unusual excitement was visible about the houses grouped around the stack-yard, and after listening a few moments to see if anyone, alarmed by the cries, approached the spot, he turned again to his companion with a sigh of relief.

Sarah had fallen upon her back, and as he bent over to lift her up, her pale face shone strangely white in the dim starlight.

Could it be death? he thought. *No!* She was yet alive, and the pallor which so startled him was the whiteness of a swoon.

The sight of her lying there so still and white, unconscious of all passing around her, led his thoughts into strange channels, and his face lit up with a gleam of devilish ferocity. His breath came in hurried gasps, and his brain reeled in a delirium of frenzy. He turned, as though animated by a sudden purpose, and strode through the bushes and over the rough, stony ground with swift strides.

Against the distant horizon loomed up the shadowy outline of a farm wagon. It was directly in his path, he stopped before it, and leaning over the side lifted a cloth or bag which lay in the bottom, and in nervous haste began to tear it apart.

This will do, he thought, holding up a piece of twine—*it is hemp and strong as a cable.*

He threw the remainder of the bag back into the wagon, and with the string in his hand, he started back toward the haystack. As he passed through the bushes, a trailing bramble caught his cloak and detained him for a moment. With a fierce curse, he tore himself loose, and with such strength, he reeled madly. He heard some-thing fall and strike with a sharp ring on the frozen ground. He turned back to search for it and groped blindly among the bushes and briars with his naked hands. Whatever it was, he wouldn't find it, and again, he started.

Reaching the haystack, he lightly vaulted the fence, raising the body of the fainting girl, throwing back her head, and passing the cord he held in his hand twice around her white neck. Seizing the two ends, he crossed them and drew the loop together with all his strength. Startled, the girl opened her eyes. He drew the string tighter. She struggled faintly, gasped once or twice, and beat the air with her hands, as though to tear away the thongs that kept out God's pure air and caused strange lights and the most horrible phantasmagoria to flit through her brain. In vain. The cruel string clasped her neck the tighter, and with a final shudder, her hands were dropped to her side, and her head fell back.

The murderer had accomplished his work, and he only needed to destroy all traces of his crime! He dropped the body and began to unlace the dead girl's shoes. He lifted the corpse, already assuming rigidity, and made the cord fast about her neck. He reached up and tied the other end to a stake leaning against the haystack. As he raised her in his arms, her long hair fell and veiled her sweet face from the unholy gaze of the murderer. Folding up her clothes smoothly under her knees and lifting her feet from the ground, he placed the shoes together and set them down near her body. Then, with a last look around him to see that no eye looked upon him, he vaulted the fence and plunged down the road toward Howland's Bridge.

The ghastly object hanging against the stack grew colder and more rigid. The long hair floated back and forth on the night breeze, and the gray December dawn ushered into the light of day all that remained to witness the terrible deed.

~ 8 ~

THE MURDERER TAKES FLIGHT

After leaving the haystack, Avery shaped his course in the direction of Howland's Bridge, intending to reach Portsmouth if possible before midnight. He could take the ferry from there to Bristol. He had occasion in the course of his walk to require his handkerchief, but after a diligent search, he could not find it and thought he might have lost it somewhere in the hurry to escape. It was an ordinary red bandana, and there was no mark on it by which it could be identified.

When he reached Portsmouth, it was past nine o'clock, and not caring to disturb any of his friends, he went to the only hotel in the place, kept by one Jeremiah Gilford, who also owned the ferry, and, finding everything dark, knocked loudly for admission. He tried the front door for a while and then went around to the rear of the house. His efforts here were more successful than in front, for after pounding vigorously for several minutes, footsteps were heard on the inside, and the proprietor, evidently just from his bed, opened the door and peered cautiously out.

"Who's there?" He said, not at first seeing Avery.
"It's me!" replied the preacher, stepping forward. "How do you do it, Mr. Gifford?"
"Oh, it's you!" said Gifford. "Come in." Thus invited, Avery came

into the room and approached the fireplace, which burned a cheerful fire.

"It's late," observed the hotelkeeper, setting down his candle and
locking the door.

Avery looked up from the fire and remarked, "Not as late as you
think. Can you take me across the ferry tonight?"

"No, sir! It will be impossible to take you across before morning."

"I have been up the island on business, said Avery. "Brother Warren
told me I could cross the ferry at any time. If I had known I could
not cross, I would not have disturbed you but would have kept on
to my brother Cook's and spent the night there."

"As for that, elder, you can have a bed here, and I will take you
across early in the morning."

"No, no! But you may give me a drink of water if you will. One of my
family members is unwell, and I am anxious to get home as soon as
possible."

"You'd better stay, elder," persisted Gifford. "It's a cold night, and
it's a long walk to Cook's."

"I don't know, but you are right," replied Avery after considering
for a moment. "I guess I'll stay."

Gifford took up the candle and, bidding his guests to follow him,
led the way upstairs. They passed a clock in the entry, and Gifford
observed that it was fifteen minutes after ten o'clock. He ushered
the minister into an unoccupied chamber and, bidding him good-
night, sought his own bed. Avery was up before sunrise, and after
a hasty breakfast, he was carried across by ferry by Gifford's son,
William. On the way across, the young man turned to the preacher
and said:

"I did not know you were going to preach last evening, elder."

"And I did not," replied Avery. "I was up to my brother Cook's expertise."

"Oh!" exclaimed the young man, and he relapsed into silence.

Safely across, Avery breathed freer, and just as people were beginning to stir and begin the business of the day, he entered his own house and went directly to bed.
He had a terrible ordeal to pass through in the next few days, but he had studied his part well and bore up under all the direct evidence hurled against him with fortitude and bravery that, had he been innocent, would have been worthy of a Spartan.

He had no lack of friends, and the result of the trial showed how well they stood by him. With the majority of them, it was not because he was a minister of the Methodist Church and was being wrongfully persecuted that they defended him, for no sane man could have doubted his guilt despite his fervent protestations of innocence; but it was Brother Avery, the godlike, the saintly, the eloquent, who was accused of murder, and he must be acquitted at any cost, even if perjured testimony was necessary.

After his apprehension and before his release on bail to remain confined to his own house, secret meetings were held nightly by the members of his church, and under the guise of pious condolence with their pastor in his dire distress, they hatched a plan for his acquittal and release worthy of the arch-fiends in hell.

Something must be done to rebut the strong evidence of his guilt and to offset the strenuous efforts being made by the citizens of Fall River to have justice done. The country was scoured in search of witnesses, not overly scrupulous or nice, who would swear to any story that might be taught them. Money was raised to defray the expenses of the trial, to employ the best legal talent, to buy and bribe, and the Fall River people began to fear that they had been too lenient with the priestly murderer and to wish that without trial by jury or sentence by judge, they had strictly administered the Old Mosaic Law, which gave an eye for an eye, a tooth for a tooth, and a life for a life. So strong was the feeling against Avery, and so much were the people displeased with the lenient manner in which he had been treated, that a large crowd besieged his house Christmas morning and demanded that he be delivered over into their hands to receive the punishment he so richly deserved—death!

It is perhaps no more than justice to this mob to say that had Avery fallen into their hands, he would have been dealt with as justly as though he had been arraigned before a regular tribunal. They thought it unfair that he should be examined in his town by magistrates of his selection who were members of his church and his friends. They argued, and with reason, that, had he been taken into the county where the crime was committed and examined there, he would have been remanded to jail to await trial instead of being released on bail. They simply demanded justice, and from appearances, it seemed that they meant to have it.

At the approach of the crowd, Avery, surrounded by several of his most intimate friends, and hence his most fanatical partisans, retreated to an upstairs room and, standing beside the window, surveyed the excited crowd below. Determined faces glared up at him, and he trembled for his life. "Won't somebody go down and—pacify—try to induce them to leave?" he said, with a beseeching look at his friends.

However, nobody volunteered as he paced back and forth across the room with nervous strides, periodically walking over to the window to look down upon the crowd. Suddenly he stopped, and all color forsook his face as a crash was heard below, like the bursting of a door or shutter, and the heavy tramp of many feet over the kitchen floor told the scared men above that the mob had effected an entrance.

Below the stairs, the noise grew louder, and angry words, mingled with imprecations and curses on the head of the man of whom they were in search, were heard. One of the party members in the room, bolder than the rest, opened the door and went downstairs. The room was full of men; from their dress and manner evidently work people, and to one who seemed to be the leader, he addressed himself:

"What do you want?" He said, still standing on the stairs and holding the door, but a little way open.

"We want the preacher!" replied the man, and the crowd echoed his words, "Yea, the preacher! We want the murderer!"

"But, gentlemen," said Avery's friend, at that minute catching a glimpse of Deputy Sheriff Paul, "you can't have him."

"But we'll take him!" persisted the mob, crowding about him. "He won't escape. We'll hang him!"

"Mr. Paul, cried the man, still holding the door. Will you allow us to be murdered? Can you not pacify these men?"

It is doubtful whether the deputy sheriff expressed his thoughts on the matter when he replied, "But he is a sworn officer of the law and must do his duty."

"You will be protected," he said, and then, turning to the crowd harangued them at some length. After some time, they filed slowly out, but it was evident they were not satisfied, and many lingered about the house until nightfall.

Deputy Sheriff Paul, accompanied by the steamboat engineer, Orswell, went upstairs, and after his companion had positively identified Avery as the man from whom he had received the letter, left to return to Fall River. When the crowd had thinned down to a few stragglers, the preacher ventured downstairs to eat his supper.

Fearing that if he didn't remain in the house, the men might return and hang him to the nearest tree, he begged his friends to either stay with him, or take him to a place of safety, and until after the examination, he remained hidden. When he was finally released on bail, he broke the stipulation on the recognition and, aided by these same friends, left Bristol under cover of darkness, and by circuitous routes, traveling only at night, at last, reached the house of a friend in Rindge, New Hampshire.

~ 9 ~

EPHRAIM AVERY REARRESTED

When it became generally known that Avery had fled the state, the people of Fall River were highly incensed, and a party was at once organized to ferret him out and bring him back to justice. Although he had disguised himself as much as possible by shaving and cutting his hair, he was tracked to his hiding place and re-arrested. They found him concealed in the house of Mr. Mayo, who was prominently connected with the Methodist church, and although Avery contended that he could not be arrested without a requisition and objected very strongly to being taken back to Rhode Island, they satisfied him that they were proceeding in the matter legally and brought him back to be tried.

On January 28th, the body of the murdered girl was exhumed and examined for evidence of an abortion attempt. Dissection indicated that such an attempt had been made, and the government, with this new evidence in its possession, seemed confident in convicting the prisoner.

Slowly the time slipped by, and, despite the powerful combination organized to defeat the ends of justice, the grand jury presented a bill of indictment against Avery, and at the session of the Supreme Judicial Court, Holden at Newport, within and for the county of Newport, on the first Monday of March,1833, he was arrested, and through his counsel pleaded not guilty. The time elapsing since the commission of the crime had enabled Avery to get full command of his faculties, and he came into court and seated himself near his counsel with a jaunty air of triumph.

The sixth day of May was assigned by the court for the trial, and Avery was then remanded. On the day in question, on the re-assembling of the court, Samuel Eddy, Chief Justice, presiding, Charles Brayton, and Job Durfee, associates, on motion of Albert C. Greene, Esq., Attorney-General, the prisoner was brought into court.

As he marched forward to the dock, closely guarded by two deputy sheriffs, all eyes were upon him, and a murmur of sullen rage arose from the throng of men, women, and children crowded into the courtroom. The restless eyes of the prisoner wandered about the room and then sank to the ground. He took his seat, and after a moment, he gained confidence and lifted his eyes.

The Attorney-General moved that a venire be ordered to summon forty-eight jurors, in addition to the fourteen already drawn. These jurors are to be in court at nine o'clock on Tuesday morning.

Richard K. Randolph, Esq., one of the counsels for the prisoner, moved "that such gentlemen as might be in court taking notes be prohibited from causing the same to be published, until after the verdict of the jury be rendered," and extraordinary as such a request may be considered by the people of today, enjoying all the benefits of email, and TV, it was so ordered!

Promptly at eleven o'clock, the court opened and the prisoner entered, a little paler than the day before, as though the excitement and suspense of the trial were beginning to wear on him.

After the calling of the jury, the clerk read the indictment and, turning to Avery, addressed him as follows:

"Ephraim K. Avery, to this indictment you have already pleaded not guilty—what say you now?"

The prisoner rose slowly to his feet and, raising his eyes, replied in a low voice: "Not guilty!"

"How will you be tried?"

Avery's admirable self-possession and mental control were coming to his rescue, and his reply to this question was given confidently and in a louder tone of voice:

"By God and my country!"

"God send you a good deliverance!" cried the clerk, and the court then ordered the jurors to be called.

All the remainder of the day was spent getting a jury. Six only were obtained by this panel, and the court therefore ordered another venire to issue six new jurors and adjourned until Wednesday at three p.m.

The court re-assembled at three p.m. on Wednesday, and the business of getting a jury continued. Forty-four of the last panel were gone through before twelve men, "good and true," were found.

After the jury was sworn in, the prisoner was called, and the indictment was read.

"To this indictment, the prisoner has pleaded not guilty," said the clerk, "and for trial, he has put himself upon God and his country, which country, gentlemen of the jury, you are. Hear the evidence!"

After this, there was some legal sparring over the question of an adjournment, and the court, to end the matter, adjourned until the next morning

~ 10 ~

THE 1ST, 2ND & 3RD DAYS OF TRIAL

The First Day of Trial

Monday, May the 6th

Shortly after the opening of the first day of trial when the Judges and counsel had taken their seats, the prisoner was brought in. He bowed to each, and sat at the counsel table with perfect self-possession, which was not however characterized by any unbecoming confidence of demeanor, but appeared rather the result of great mental firmness.

In point of health, he seems to have suffered severely since his arraignment last March; his face might almost be described as cadaverous. After the prisoner had been seated, the Clerk of Court read aloud the names of the Counsel for the state and the defense. The Counsel for the State in this prosecution are:

- General Albert C. Green, Attorney General;
- The Honorary J. D. Pearce of Newport,
- William R. Staples, Esq. of Providence,
- Those retained for the prisoner are:
- Richard K. Randolph, Esq. of Newport;
- the Honorary Jeremiah Mason, of Boston;

- J. Turner, Esq., and Henry Y. Cranston, Esq., both of Newport;
- and Samuel Blake, Esq. of Bristol

Attorney-General: "If it pleases the court, I move that the trial of the prisoner proceed; or, if this be now impracticable, that a time be assigned for it."

Chief Justice: "As far as we are concerned there is no objection; and if there is none on the part of the prisoner, the Clerk can proceed immediately to call the jury."

Mr. Randolph (for the prisoner): "I feel somewhat embarrassed at the difficulty which I anticipate will be found in the formation of a jury for the trial of this case, and therefore submit it to the court, whether, in this particular instance, it would not be proper to form a panel at large; and from parts of the county distant from each other, to obviate, if possible, the difficulty which may arise."

Chief Justice—"It may be expedient to enlarge the present panel: but we can give no order as to forming it from particular towns or places, for this must be left to the discretion of the Sheriff."

A venire (jury pool) was accordingly issued for the addition of forty-eight jurors to the present panel of fifteen; and of this aggregate, the prisoner will be entitled to twenty peremptory challenges.

The Second Day of Trial

Tuesday, May the 7th

The Judges having taken their seals at 9 o'clock, the Attorney General moved that the prisoner be brought into Court. He was brought in, and he took his seat as before at the table near his Counsel. He appeared feverish and somewhat less composed than yesterday. He was dressed in a black vest, pantaloons, and an overcoat nearly the same color; on his face, he wore purple spectacles.

Clerk of Court—"Ephraim K. Avery, hold up your hand."

He held it up briefly, then placed it in the breast of his coat, leaving his left on the back of a chair. The fearful indictment was then read. The first Count charged him with having, at Tiverton, in the county of Newport, fastened a cord around the neck of Sarah Maria Cornell, and therewith choked and strangled her; the 2nd that he therewith strangled her, and hung her to a stake; and the 3d, that he struck and beat her upon the lower part of the belly, in and upon the left side, and upon the back; inflicting mortal strokes and bruises; and that he place the cord aforesaid round her neck, and therewith did violently constrict, compress and squeeze her neck until she died.

As on his first arraignment, he preserved unruffled composure, unless indeed his actively and incessantly chewing some small substance, apparently white paper, may be considered an involuntary mechanical indication of a strongly condensed mental agony which his firmness would not allow to be less equivocally expressed. His deep blue eyes intensely fixed on the Clerk of the Court during the whole time the indictment was being read, seemed to gather a yet more vivid intensity whenever a detail particularly horrible caught his ear. Yet, his appearance, to a superficial observer, is calculated to excite respect, and in his manner, there is nothing that the most prejudiced could charge with impropriety.

Clerk of the Court: "How say you prisoner, Guilty? or not Guilty?"

Prisoner: "Not Guilty Sir!" he said firmly, and with an emphatic motion of the head.

Clerk—"How will you be tried?"

Prisoner: "By God and my country!" He replied with a devotional intonation.

Clerk—"May God send you a good deliverance."

He was then directed in the usual form to challenge the Jurors as they should come to be sworn in.

Attorney General: The course, until now, adopted in this Court, on each capital trial has been to put each juror on his voire dire (the preliminary examination of a juror). The first juror called was Abraham Barker—to whom the Attorney General asked the following three questions, as he did to each of the others:

1. *Are you related either to the prisoner or to the deceased?*
2. *Have you any conscientious scruples to finding a man guilty of a crime which the law punishes with death?*
3. *Have you formed or expressed any opinion of the guilt or innocence of the prisoner?*

The application of these questions gave rise to discussions between the opposing counsel, which were renewed throughout the day, and appeared interminable. The Honorary Jeremiah Mason, & Mr. Randolph, of counsel for the prisoner contended by arguments and authorities, that the last question should distinctly elicit whether the opinion which the juror may have formed or expressed was against the prisoner, instead of the general answer that he had formed or expressed an opinion. They said that unless they knew whether that opinion was against the prisoner they could not know when to challenge a juror. The Court stated that the rule of practice established in this State, was, that when a juror had formed an opinion, either for or against a prisoner, he was equally disqualified for the impartial exercise of his solemn duty, and was, therefore, to be "challenged for the cause." The Attorney General defended this principle with great clearness; but the Hon. J. Mason, having cited from the Massachusetts Reports the use of the separate inter-rogatory "have you formed any bias against the prisoner," the Court deemed it an authority, and expressed their inclination to adopt, in the present peculiar ease, the practice of that State. But the Attorney General, having felt himself authorized by this prac-tice, to pursue the further question "Would that bias incapacitate you to render an impartial verdict after hearing the testimony, the counsel for the prisoner objected; and the discussion which ensued, indicating no tendency to a conclusion before it should become merged in the business of the Supreme Tribunal of the human race, the Court took a (welcome) recess for the lunch hour, and stated that they would rule the question at 3 o'clock, that afternoon. Only three jurors were sworn this forenoon, out of 48 who were either challenged for the cause or peremptorily by the prisoner.

At 3 o'clock, the Judges resumed their seats, and the Court ruled that they would adhere to the established practice of this state, viz: that if a juror declared he had formed or expressed an opinion of the guilt or innocence of a prisoner upon a capital charge, he should be deemed disqualified.

Upon this principle, the formation of the jury was re-commenced, and at the adjournment of the Court, three more jurors had been sworn: making half the number required. The panel, from the last venire, having been exhausted a new one was issued for 60 other jurors.

The Third Day of Trial

Wednesday, May the 8th

The Court did not sit until 3, P.M. to allow time for the arrival of jurors. The remainder of the day was occupied as the day preceding, but with the gratifying result that six more jurors had been sworn: thus making the required number. The Court considering the hour at which this desideratum was obtained too late to open the cause with convenience, adjourned until the morning.

The following are the names of the Jury: Eleazer Trevett, Foreman; Joseph Martin, Charles Lawton, George Tilley, Horatio Taylor, Noah Barker, James Easton, William Read, Gideon Peckham, Milton Hall, Edwin Wilbor, John Sherman.

The whole number of jurors challenged on this trial by the Court and the prisoner was 108; by the prisoner alone, nine.

The formation of this jury, perhaps unprecedented for its difficulty in this state and in many others, was distinguished in its progress by some remarkable peculiarities. One is, that of the whole number of jurors challenged but one intimated that he had formed an opinion favorable to the accused. Except for those few disqualified by conscientious scruples against returning a verdict which would ensure the punishment of death nearly the whole number called confessed to having a bias against him. Another singular fact is, that he peremptorily challenged no juror who had not explicitly declared himself strictly neutral; and many of the jurors whom he rejected, expressed their neutrality much less equivocally than several of those to whom he did not object. The rule or motive of choice between these neutral jurors, by which, under the direction of his counsel, he was guided, appeared to be the subject of much speculative opinion.

~ 11 ~

THE 4TH, 5TH, & 6TH DAYS OF TRIAL

Testimonies for the Prosecution

At the opening of the court on Thursday, the fourth day of the trial, the courtroom was crowded to suffocation, the audience being composed of two diverse elements—the factory operatives from Fall River and the members of Avery's church in Bristol.

Dutee J. Pearce, Esq., opened the case by saying that, although the indictment that had been read to the jury contained three counts, the charge against the prisoner was murder, and if he was convicted on either of the three, the verdict would be substantially the same. After saying that under the statutes of Rhode Island, the crime of murder was punishable by death, he recapitulated what would be proven by the evidence for the prosecution.

The government would prove to the jury that on the morning of December 21, 1832, the body of Sarah Maria Cornell was found dead, hanging from a stake near a haystack on the land of John Durfee in Tiverton, about half a mile from the village of Fall River. It would be proven to them that she left her boarding house in Fall River the evening before, in good health, and for her, in uncommonly good spirits; that distance from the place where she hung were circumstances to indicate a struggle and to satisfy the jury that she owed her death to some other hand than her own.

The question would naturally arise: who was the author of her death? If the prosecution could show the jury, upon this point, a previous intimacy between the prisoner and the deceased, and if her situation, caused by Avery), was such as might furnish him with an inducement to commit the act; if, on the day of the murder, the local situation of the prisoner was such that he might have committed the deed; if on the afternoon of the 20th of December, a very cold day, he left home, without giving any reason, or stating his designs to any one, and if the reasons subsequently given by him were proved to be inconsistent and absurd; if from Bristol ferry, at 2 o'clock p. m., he was traced by an indirect route to Howland's ferry bridge; if, from Lawton's house, near the bridge, he was traced by an indirect road to Fall River; if from Fall River he was brought back again, along a bypath to the stack; if from there he was carried back again to the Bristol ferry; if further evidence of violence from screams heard near the place where the body was found, were given; if, in addition to all this, there was shown that by a correspondence between the deceased and the prisoner, this very place of meeting had been agreed upon; if the parties were thus brought together, and thus prove a murder committed, the prosecution would submit to the jury that the prisoner at the bar must have been the author of the murder.

John Durfee, the first witness examined for the prosecution, testified to the finding of the body hanging from the haystack on the morning of Friday, the 21st of December. He approached her to see if she was dead and called several of his companions for assistance. The body was cut down. He described the position of the shoes and identified the handkerchief found near them. He went for the coroner and also brought away Miss Cornell's trunk and bandbox from her boarding house. In the bandbox, he found four letters and a piece of paper, which he delivered to the coroner's jury. He further stated that on the day before the murder, just before sunset, as he was driving his cattle into the barnyard, he saw a strange man about twenty rods (110 yards) from the stack where the body was found. The man was tall, had on a dark-colored coat and cape, and a black hat with a high crown and large brim. He did not see the man's face.

William Durfee was on the jury for the inquest. He examined the cord around the neck of the deceased. It was deeply embedded. The knot was under her right ear, and the cord passed twice around her neck. The knot was what farmers call two half-hitches, and sailors call it a clove hitch.

Seth Darling lived at Fall River, saw the body in the stackyard, and described its appearance and the peculiarity of the knot with which she was hanged. He sometimes acted as an assistant postmaster at Fall River. He made up the mail for Bristol on Monday morning, the 19th of November, 1832. It contained only one letter. The letterbox stood near him, open while he was making up the mail. He heard some letters drop and took out two. One was directed to South Woodstock, Connecticut, to Mr. Grindall Rawson (a letter being shown witness, he thought it the same, and that the postage marked on it, "10," in figures, was his hand); the other was for Bristol and directed to Rev. Mr. Avery.

Elihu Hicks, the coroner of Tiverton, testified to holding the inquest and to the appearance of the body.

Dr. Foster Hooper examined the body and testified to its being bruised in several places. He examined the body for the second time on the 28th of January, and from the appearance of the womb and the abdominal muscles, it should be inferred that some hard substance had been introduced into the womb. I couldn't conclude as to the fact that it had been done to produce abortion. The fetus found in the uterus weighed about five ounces and measured about eight inches in length. Medical authorities assert that a fetus eight inches long would be three months and twenty days old.

Dr. Thomas Wilbur also examined the body. His suspicion of murder was grounded on the fact that the indentation of the cord on the neck was as near one ear as the other, that there was a contusion on her hip, bruises on her knees, as if she had been down on them, and knocks or scratches, six or eight in number, on each leg between the ankle and the knee.

Lemuel W. Briggs, postmaster at Bristol, testified that on the 19th of November, one letter was received from Fall River, on which the postage was six cents. His book showed a charge of six cents to E. K. Avery on that day. On the 12th of November, one letter was received from Fall River, and on that day, his book shows a charge of six cents against E. K. Avery.

Benjamin Manchester was present when the body was cut down. He found a piece of comb in a sort of path about eighteen or twenty rods (110 yards) from the stack. On the 20th of December, he was at work blasting about fifty rods from the stack. While in the act of running from a blast, he observed a man getting over a wall near the ledge where they were blasting. He called to the man to "look out," and he halted until the stone was done falling and then walked off. He had on a dark cloak and coat and a large hat with a broad brim. He did not see his face. He saw Avery at the Bristol examination and watched him as he came out of court. As to height, dress, and hat, he compared very well with the man seen. There was a cart standing near the stack, into which the tools were put, and the bags used to sit when drilling. The bags were sewn with twine. He compared a piece of this twine with a piece of the cord by which the girl was hung and could see no difference in size or color. A piece a yard, or a yard and a half long, might have been gotten out of the bags.

Mary D. Borden assisted in laying out the body. Down the back was a very dark bruise. On both sides of the body, there was an appearance of the prints of fingers, with the thumb presenting forward. The forepart of the body, above and below the thighs, was bruised very badly. There was a little blood on her linen. This witness was corroborated in her testimony by others.

Abner Davis saw the man near the ledge of rocks when the blasting was being done. In general appearance, he compared favorably to the prisoner.

William Hamilton was passing near the scene of the murder on the night of December 20th and heard a shrill cry, like that of a woman in distress. It came from behind Durfee's house.

Eleanor Owen, who lived at the house of Thomas Tasker, the agent of the calico works, on the edge of the Fall River, heard a noise like a person screaming on the evening of the 20th of December. The wind was from the direction of the stackyard, and the screams seemed to come from that way. It was about a quarter of seven.

William Pease, Jr., ferryman at Bristol Ferry, carried Mr. Avery across the ferry from Bristol to the island at about 2 pm on December 20th.

Jeremiah Gifford saw Mr. Avery on the Portsmouth side of the ferry, in company with the last witness. Avery came to his house that night, at about quarter after ten, and wanted to be taken across the ferry to Bristol. Finding that he could not be carried over until morning, Avery stayed with him until daybreak, when his son William took him across. Avery wore a dark coat and cloak and a black hat, large and broad-brimmed. He had neither a bundle nor a cane.

William Anthony, who lived in Portsmouth, east of the ferry house, saw a stranger on the 20th of December, in the afternoon, walking toward Tiverton. He was tall and wore a dark-colored coat.

William Carr, also residing in Portsmouth, met a man on the 20th of December, between two and three o'clock, as he was returning from Fall River in a wagon. The man answered Avery's description.

Peter Cranston, keeper of Howland's ferry bridge, testified that a man answering the description already given passed across the bridge on the afternoon of December 20th. He thought he should know the gentleman again based on the fact that he had some conversation with him. The man said he was going to Fall River. He thought he saw him at the Bristol examination. He meant Mr. Avery. He went into the courthouse and, before he was pointed out to him by anybody, identified him as the man.

Several witnesses, living along the road between the bridge and Fall River, testified to seeing a man who answered Avery's description pass on the afternoon of that day, and Gardner L. Coit, bartender at Lawton's tavern at Fall River, served supper to a man whom he now identified as Avery, at about six o'clock.

John Borden, living at Tiverton, about halfway between the ferry bridge and the Fall River, met a man at about nine o'clock on the night of the 20th of December, going in the direction of Howland's bridge. The man was tall, but it was too dark to otherwise de-scribe him.

William Gifford carried Mr. Avery across the ferry on the morning of the 21st of December, from Portsmouth to Bristol, and his sister, Jane Gifford, testified to the facts already given in the testimony of her father.

Harriet Hathaway, Miss Cornell's landlady, said Sarah left home on the 20th of December, about dusk. She said she was going to Joseph Durfee's and would return before nine. She seemed more cheerful than usual. Miss Cornell was not in the habit of being out in the evenings, except when she went to class meetings.

The testimony of Lucy Hathaway, daughter of the preceding witness, who worked in the mill with the deceased, was similar to what has already been given. In addition, she identified three letters that were shown to her as ones she had seen in Miss Cornell's possession.

~ 12 ~

THE 7TH & 8TH DAYS OF TRIAL

The Seventh Day of Trial

Monday, May the 13th

Monday, May 13th, was the seventh day of the trial, and when court opened, the crowd seemed in no way diminished. The prisoner, a little paler than when the trial began, was in his accustomed seat near his counsel and listened to the evidence with marked attention.

The first witness called was Horney Hornden, one of the committee members appointed by the citizens of Fall River to conduct the prosecution. On the Saturday evening of the first week of the trial, he called the store of Iram Smith in Fall River and asked for the remainder of the letter paper he had in his store on the 8th of December. A half sheet was among the paper, and this was compared with another half sheet (i.e., the white letter found in the trunk of the deceased), and as regarded texture, color, and the fitting together of the torn edges, the two half sheets were found to correspond exactly. They corresponded when examined through a microscope. Witnesses arrested Mr. Avery after the Bristol examination at the house of Mr. Mayo in Rindge, New Hampshire. He had disguised himself by shaving and cutting his hair.

Jeremiah Hambley, living in Fall River near the old meeting house, saw a tall man, accompanied by a woman, turn down the lane leading to the bridge on the 20th of December last evening.

Iram Smith, who kept a store in Fall River, testified that on the 8th of December, at about nine or ten o'clock in the morning, Mr. Avery was in his store and asked for writing paper. It was furnished for him, and he used a half sheet. The other half-sheet was handed over by a witness to Colonel Hornden.

Jeremiah Howland was in the store as a last witness on December 8th. Mr. Avery was also present. He heard Avery call for paper and saw him with some in his hand behind the counter at the desk.

Stephen Bartlett, driving the stage from Fall River to Bristol, drove Mr. Avery home on the 8th of December. He got on the stage at the Lawton door and came from the direction of the post office. John Orswell, the engineer of the steamboat King Philip, running from Providence to Fall River, identified the red letter found in the trunk of Miss Cornell as one he had first seen at Providence in the hands of Mi. Avery. It was in the latter part of November, and the letter was put in the hands of a witness to deliver to Miss Cornell by a man whom he was certain was Avery. The letter was directed to the care of Mrs. Cole.

Elijah Cole received the letter from Orswell to be delivered to Miss Cornell, who was boarding with him at the time. While Miss Cornell lived with him, she conducted herself in a respectable manner.

Betsey E. Cole, daughter of the preceding witness, remembered the red letter. It was received on the 27th of November.

At this point, the attorney general offered to put into the case the three letters found in the trunk of the deceased. But this being opposed by the prisoner's counsel, the matter was postponed till the morning.

John J. Paine, now living in Providence, first met Miss Cornell at Woodstock in May 1832. She was living with her brother-in-law, Mr. Rawson. Witnesses carried her to the camp meeting at Thompson in August last year. He saw a considerable amount of Miss Cornell while she was at Mr. Rawson's. Her manner and demeanor were modest.

Nancy Rawson, the sister of Miss Cornell, testified to the latter's visiting the camp meeting at Thompson. Eight days before the camp meeting, she was unwell. She left their house on the 2nd of October, and at the regular time, on the contrary of the previous month. She told the witness what she feared might be her condition.

The 8th Day of Trial

Tuesday, May the 14th

On Tuesday morning, the attorney general, according to his notice given the day before, offered to put in the letters found in the trunk of the deceased. The red letter was offered first, and after considerable argument, it was admitted. Mr. Randolph, of counsel for the prisoner, asked if the jury were to presume it was Avery's letter. Chief Justice Eddy said the jury was to draw their conclusions. It was admitted merely as a paper found in her possession. The attorney general then offered the white letter. It was objected to by counsel for the prisoner, but the chief justice thought that it might be read to the jury as a matter tending to rebut the presumption of suicide. The yellow letter was then offered but not admitted, after which the slip of paper found in Miss Cornell's trunk was read to the jury.

Bailey Borden and his wife, Mary D. Borden, met Miss Cornell in company with a man, who in every particular resembled the prisoner, on Spring Street, Fall River, near the old meeting house, on the evening of the 20th of October, about half past nine.

Margaret B. Handy lived at Lawton's hotel in Fall River on the 20th of December. A stranger took supper there that night alone. He was about as tall as the preacher and resembled him in every feature. Two other people, one a pedlar, took supper together a little after.

Grindall Rawson testified as before related and spoke of the deceased as one who had always borne a good character, so far as he knew. She conducted herself properly while she was a resident at his house. She accused Mr. Avery of being the cause of her trouble. Being shown the slip of paper found in Miss Cornell's bandbox, he identified it as her handwriting.

John Boyd, residing in Portsmouth, had some conversation with Mr. Avery shortly after the examination began in Bristol as to his whereabouts on the 20th of December. Avery said he came over the ferry, went directly up the road, and got over the wall near the mill. Witnesses could not say whether there was a little on this side or beyond. He then steered off in about a southwest direction, till he came to a brook or rivulet. Near the brook, he saw a man with a gun and had some conversation with him. He also met a boy, with whom he also conversed.

Lucy Spink saw a man who resembled a prisoner in company with Miss Cornell on the 20th of October.

Sarah S. Jones lived in Portsmouth, and on the 20th of December, she saw a stranger pass her house in the forenoon. She had a conversation with Mr. Avery on this subject at his house. He inquired about the appearance of the man and the direction he took. He told her not to repeat in court that he had inquired about her. Mr. Bullock was present. In the entry, coming down, Mr. Avery told her his life was worth thousands of worlds and depended on her evidence.

Rufus H. Lesore was a clerk in the post office at Fall River in November and December 1832. He recalled delivering a letter to S. M. Cornell, marked one cent postage. The letter was dropped on the same day he delivered it. The man who dropped it in resembled the prisoner.

The attorney-general here stated that the evidence for the government was closed.

~ 13 ~

LYING TO PROVE THE EVIDENCE FALSE

The 9th Day of Trial

Wednesday, May the 15th

The case was opened for defense on the afternoon of the ninth day by Richard K. Randolph, Esq., in a long speech in which he questioned the veracity of the testimony offered by the prosecution and attempted to prove that the death of S. M. Cornell was a suicide. He would prove that the knot was one used by weavers in mending the harness on their loom and that the fact that the string by which she was hanged was so short was nothing at all. The government witnesses had all said that the cloak worn by Miss Cornell was so far unhooked that she might have fastened the rope with her own hands, and once fastened, even allowing the knot to be a clove hitch, a sudden pull would have drawn it as tight as it was. He ridiculed the assumption that the paper found in the girl's bandbox was sufficient ground to suspect murder and treated the evidence of the medical experts as mere theory, without any foundation of fact to support it. He would prove that the deceased often threatened to commit suicide and that, from the general singularity of her conduct, it could be surmised that she was insane. He would show the whole history of the girl for the last fourteen years; her character wherever she had resided had been bad, and taking her confession, Avery could not be the father of her child. He would prove that Mr. Avery could not possibly have been the man who delivered the red letter to Orswell and that several of the other important witnesses would be confronted with proof of their perjury. As to where Avery went on the afternoon of the death, he would show that he took exactly the course testified to by the government's witness, Boyd, and that he did meet the man and the boy, as he said. Unfortunately for Mr. Avery, however, that man and boy could not be found. The fact of Avery's "fleeing from justice" and "disguising himself" could be easily accounted for.

The first witnesses called were medical men, mostly from distant cities, to disprove the evidence of Doctors Hospital and Wilbur. These scientists were unanimous in the opinion that the fetus found was, from its size, at least five months old and that the bruises found were not bruises at all, but the natural results of decay. Other medical men followed, who testified that they had been called upon by Miss Cornell for the treatment of a loathsome disease, which was of long-standing, and that from her conversation at these consultations, they judged her to be a lewd woman.

After this came a mass of testimony, which was undoubtedly purchased, for, although the observations extended over some twelve or fifteen years, they were unanimous in the opinion that Miss Cornell was insane, and according to them, she had attempted suicide a score of times from remorse at being so utterly lost to all morality that decent, respectable people would not associate with her.

The next act in this remarkable drama was constructed differently. At least one hundred good methods came forward and verified that when the camp meeting took place at Thompson, Mr. Avery was never in the company of Miss Cornell—no, not for a single moment. Others, of the same stripe, remembered to have noticed the appearance of Miss Cornell at this time and to also have a recollection, just at this particular crisis, of having mentioned their suspicions to others of the saintly brethren and sisters and to have remarked that if Miss Cornell was not married, she had better do so at once and save herself the disgrace that her appearance indicated.

While the audience was in a daze over the preceding revelations, another attack was made, and another crowd of witnesses flocked to the front to testify that none of the government's principal witnesses were to be believed for a minute, arid to swear that what they had already testified was false in every particular and that the story they were about to tell was the only genuine account.

For every fact that had been proven by the government, the defense offered evidence in rebuttal—Methodist evidence. Good men, who bore excellent characters for honesty and integrity, came forward to the stand and swore to anything to save Brother Avery, and women, who before had held it to be a cardinal sin to tell a false-hood, swore to undoubted lies rather than see their beloved fellow laborer in Christ hung.

The reader who thinks it rather improbable that Christian men and women should thus perjure themselves has evidence and over-whelming evidence of what man will do under the influence of re-ligion—or shall we call it fanaticism?—in the case of a more recent date. The world stood aghast when men and women, holding the highest social positions and of the very highest moral character, came forward in the Beecher-Tilton imbroglio and perjured them-selves unblushingly. Hundreds were found who would not only allow a lie to go down to posterity as sworn evidence unchallenged but were also willing, yes, anxious, to tabulate fresh falsehoods to bind those already told and swear to the truth of both.

It would be impossible to give even a synopsis of the evidence offered by the defense in this pamphlet, but it can be summed up in a few sentences. Mr. Avery was a saint of the purest, most godlike type, and Miss Cornell was not only deranged but also a wanton, a liar, and a thief. On the day of the camp meeting, Avery was not out of sight of these lynx-eyed guardians of his character for a single moment, and he could not possibly have had any collusion with Miss Cornell. He had never met her by appointment at the times sworn to by the witnesses for the prosecution, and on the day of the murder, he was in a direction the opposite of where he had been seen, and at the hour when it was presumed the murder was committed, when the screams were heard, he was at least six miles away! From noon on Wednesday, May 15th, until Friday morning, May 31st, the examination of witnesses was carried out, and so admirably had the plot to defeat justice been hatched and so skillfully carried out that the government could not rebut one of the glaring perjuries. On Saturday, June 1st, Counselor Mason, who had summed up for the defense, sat down after a glowing oration that had continued the greater part of the day, confident that the case was theirs.

The attorney general, in summarizing for the government, made but a feeble effort. The evidence in the rebuttal had been so overwhelming that he felt certain in his mind that the case was lost. He could only maintain that the evidence offered by the defense was false and fabricated. He had intended to present to them the evidence fairly on behalf of the government, and that duty, to the best of his ability, he had discharged. It remained for the jury to discharge theirs and to look to it that, whoever else might be satisfied or dissatisfied with their verdict, or whatever the ultimate result might be, they might be able to say that what they did, they did under a deep sense of their responsibility to the state, to the prisoner, and their God!

~ 14 ~

THE ACQUITTAL

Chief Justice Eddy's Charge to the Jury

The silence of several minutes fell upon the crowded courtroom after the attorney-general had finished speaking, and the relief was welcome when the venerable chief justice turned on the bench and began to address the jury. He said:

Gentlemen of the Jury: This case furnishes but little matter that requires any instruction from the court. Until a late period, it has not been the custom for the courts of this state to charge juries at all. The recent statute by which this duty is imposed has not been construed to extend to that summing up of the evidence common in other states but only to instructions in points of law.

It may be necessary to state to you that the paper in pencil marks, read in the course of the trial, was admitted for a special purpose, viz., to rebut the suspicion of suicide, and you are to use it as evidence to that point and no other.

The white letter was originally admitted under a similar restriction, but evidence has since been offered, which makes it appropriate for you, should you consider that evidence strong enough to fix the authorship of it upon the prisoner, to receive this letter as general evidence upon the issue.

Various passages have been read to you from a book of authority on the doctrine of circumstantial evidence, which I don't need to recapitulate. The substance of them seems to be that this sort of evidence is to be construed with sound discretion according to the dictates of common sense. All the circumstances relied upon must be consistent with themselves, with the hypotheses sought to be established, and inconsistent with any other.

I should recommend to you that you consider, in the first place, the question of suicide, because if you think that to have been the cause of the death, you need to go no further. If you think the death was not suicide, you can next inquire if it was caused by the prisoner.

I need not caution you to free yourselves from all feelings other than that of a desire to do justice, for, from the tenor of your oaths and the examination to which you were subjected, I have no right to suppose you are under the influence of any partiality. But I will recommend to you that you proceed with the grave duty now incumbent upon you with coolness, caution, candor, and deliberation.

If you think the defendant is guilty, you will say so; if not guilty, you will return a verdict of acquittal. I ought to add that if there is reasonable doubt in your mind, that doubt is in the prisoner's favor.

After the chief justice had finished speaking, Mr. Sergeant Tripp was sworn in, and the jury committed his charge. After remaining in session until 7 p.m., the court separated to meet at the ringing of the bell whenever the jury might agree.

All night the crowd watched the courthouse, and the church bells of that sunshiny Sabbath morning called but few worshippers together. The prisoner had been conveyed back to the jail, and all through the weary hours of that terrible night, he paced the floor of his narrow cell, ears keenly alert for the signal, which was to decide for him liberty or death! Moments seemed to lengthen into hours and hours into days, and that weary morning was recalled by him years later, as one he would look back over an interminable stretch of years. At last, it came, and the prisoner, the jury, the judges, and the crowd once again took their positions.

"Gentlemen of the jury, have you agreed upon your verdict?" asked the clerk, dipping his pen in the ink and bending toward them.

"We have!" replied the jurors as one man. "Who shall speak for you?" again queried the clerk.

"Our Foreman."

"Mr. Foreman, what say you, is the prisoner at the bar guilty or not guilty?"

A silence as of death fell upon the assembly, and the prisoner leaned forward and clutched the back of a chair in the intensity of his emotional suspense. The foreman rose slowly to his feet and, looking squarely at the prisoner, replied:

"Not guilty!"

"Gentlemen of the jury, as your foreman has said, what do you all say?" said the clerk, and the court officers in vain attempted to silence the outburst of indignation that arose and threatened to break into a riot as the verdict was rendered, and the answers of the jurors could hardly be heard.

"We do."

The clerk paused for a minute until the tumult had, in a measure, subsided, and then continued in a voice of great solemnity:

"Gentlemen of the jury, hearken to your verdict as the court has recorded it. You say the prisoner is not guilty. Is that your verdict?"

"It is," was the answering chorus, and again arose cries of indignation from the crowd of workmen and workwomen in the body of the room.

The acquitted turned his head slightly to survey the throng, and a hundred faces glaring at him over the railing were so expressive of vindictive hatred that he involuntarily shuddered and drew nearer to his counsel as if to put himself outside the protecting arm of the law.

"I move that the defendant be discharged," said Counselor Randolph at length.

Chief Justice Eddy glanced at the attorney general, who nodded his head in grim silence, and then said:

"Ephraim K. Avery, you are now discharged from custody and ordered to go without delay."

The late prisoner had risen to his feet, glancing nervously at the crowd, murmured a few words of thanks, and then, surrounded by the true friends whose perjured oaths had snatched him from the gallows, left the courtroom, and the great trial was at an end.

CONCLUSION

Although a jury of his peers had acquitted him, Avery did not consider it safe to longer remain in the neighborhood, and aided by his friends, who had proven so true and steadfast in their fanatical devotion, he disappeared from Bristol a few days after his discharge, and in that vicinity, he was never seen again.

It was rumored that he had gone west, and several years later, this surmise proved to be correct. With the money provided by his friends, he purchased a farm in the valley of Miami in the State of

Ohio, and here, in the peaceful pursuit of husbandry, he lived until his death.

In justice to the man and as proof that he repented of his terrible crime, it may be said in this connection that the latter portion of his life was marked by an extreme uprightness of living, which won for him the goodwill and friendship of his neighbors, and his many acts of charity are to this day a subject of remark among the people of this section of the country. The story of Sarah Cornell is perhaps forgotten, except by the older portion of the inhabitants, but among the factory folk of Fall River, the legend is yet preserved and handed down religiously from generation to generation as one of the sacred traditions of the craft. Her grave is yet pointed out to the inquiring stranger, and a spot shows where, as I said, the haystack stood where she was hanged.

~ 15 ~

SARAH MARIA CORNELL SPEAKS

Give Me That

Old-Time Religion!

As I stated In the preface, the dream I had about Blas Trujillos made me wonder about other souls who were victims of murders that were either unsolved, misclassified, or wrongly adjudicated. I did an internet search and found a list of names of murder victims dating back several centuries. As I scrolled down the list, I began to see visions of those victims who were reaching out to me. Sarah Maria Cornell was one of the first to do so. As her murder flashed before my eyes, I knew I had to tell her story.

As soon I sat down with my laptop and invited the spirit of Sarah Maria Cornell to come and tell me her story, my visions started to unfold like a modern-day motion picture. She began her story by showing me how she was seduced by the *rock star* of all Methodist ministers—Rev. Ephraim K. Avery. In my vision, I see Sarah at an old-fashioned camp-style church gathering, where many attendees had to stand because there weren't enough seats. Sarah, an attractive, petite woman just over five feet tall, was among those standing at the back of the tent. She wore a simple, light brown dress with a dark brown shawl draped over her shoulders and arms. Atop her head sat a tan-colored straw bonnet, fastened with a beige ribbon under her chin. This bonnet concealed most of her dark brown hair, except for a few short strands that hung down over her forehead. I watched as she swayed in harmony with the other attendees, joining them in singing hymns. Her rapturous movements caught the attention of Rev. Ephraim Avery, who could not avert his gaze. His lustful glances continued to fixate on her during the remainder of the service, and when the benediction had been said, he made a beeline toward her at breakneck speed.

Running up behind her, he tapped her on the shoulder. When she turned around, he introduced himself like an awkward schoolboy with a childhood crush. "Hello. My name is Ephraim. Did you like the sermon?"

With a chuckle, Sarah replied, "Sir, I know you are, and yes, I enjoyed the service. It was quite uplifting. I must leave now. Good-night, reverend."

As she turned to walk away, he grabbed her by the arm and said, "Please don't go. I would love the opportunity to talk to you more about my message and how I might improve it."

"Well, I must say that I am very honored that you would seek my opinion on such a matter, but I really don't see how I can be of any help to you. After all, don't you get your inspiration from God?"

"Of course I do, but it's important to know if my flock is being nourished by the messages I deliver. I must speak to a few other congregants. Please wait for me behind the meeting house next to the tent, and when the others have left, I will meet you there so we can talk."

I sensed her bewilderment at his request, wondering what benefit he could possibly obtain from getting her opinion. With a smile on her face, I heard her say to him, "It would be my privilege to oblige you, reverend. I will meet you there, but please hurry. I must be getting home soon."

Sarah's religious convictions were sincere. I could feel her deep love for God and her unwavering commitment to living as a virtuous Christian woman. She held Reverend Ephraim in high regard, but her devout and somewhat naive nature prevented her from realizing that he had ulterior motives. It was a sexual encounter he wanted, not her opinion.

Sarah's Rendezvous With Reverend Ephraim

As my vision continued, dusk settled over the landscape as the sun dipped below the horizon. I watched as Ephraim quickly made his way across the meadow in the direction of the meeting house, where Sarah eagerly waited for him to arrive. Thinking that she should make her way to the house before complete darkness ensued, Sarah started to walk away in the direction of home. Ephraim saw that she was leaving and called out to her to wait. She turned around and walked towards him, meeting him halfway. He took her arm in his and escorted her into the meeting house.

In the darkness, he asked her to sit down on the front pew. She did so, and he sat down beside her. After a few moments of silence, he put his arm around her waist and drew her close to him.

"There's something I've been wanting to tell you for several months. I have adored you from afar for many years. I love you and have to have you!"

She pulled away and, standing up, severely rebuked him, saying, "Reverend, this cannot be. You are a servant of God and a married man. You have a wife waiting for you at home, and I am a virtuous woman!"

"Ha, a lot, you know! What wife? My so-called wife has failed and betrayed me in every manner. I will put that adulterous wench away with a letter of divorce in the sight of God and the church. She is not the godly woman I need. She is nothing like you! I have a very high regard for you, Sarah. I love you!" He stood up, grabbed her around the waist, and pulled her body against his.

"God as my witness, I love you, and no one shall come between us!"

Drawing her face to his, he kissed her long and passionately. At first, she struggled to break away from his hold but soon gave in to his sensual kisses and lustful embrace.

Moonlight cascaded through the stained glass windows on the western side of the sanctuary, and I watched as Eddie lowered Sarah to the floor. He quickly removed her clothing and then his. Their silhouettes melded together as she surrendered to his sexual advances. The seduction was complete. He had achieved his goal. He had conquered Sarah, and she was now his trophy. Her life would never be the same again.

As my vision continued to unfold, I witnessed several more encounters between Sarah and Ephraim. They would sometimes rendezvous at a nearby hotel in a neighboring town, but most often, they met in the woods following church services. Towards the conclusion of my visions, Sarah confided in me, saying:

> Ephraim continued to seduce me for several months after our initial meeting. He spun falsehoods and made commitments he had no intention of honoring. He professed his love for me and expressed a desire to make me his wife. He vowed to marry me as soon as his divorce, sanctioned by the church, was granted. He insisted that his wife had committed adultery, though she hadn't. Once he discovered I was pregnant, he reneged on his promise, claiming that the church lacked sufficient evidence against his wife and, therefore, he

couldn't divorce her to marry me. He reassured me not to worry, asserting that he was devising a plan and would support me and our baby, provided I kept our secret.

The Betrayal

As my visions continued, I watched as Sarah walked alone. Mixed with a sense of fear and hope, her mind raced from one thought to another in anticipation of Ephraim's plan. Is he planning to elope with me to another state where we can live our lives as man and wife and raise our child together, or does he want to send me away to have and raise my baby alone? She walked a little further before reaching the rear of the old meeting house, which had served as the backdrop to many of their clandestine rendezvous.

Hiding in the shadow of darkness, stood Ephraim by the back door. He held a parcel wrapped in a red handkerchief. With a simple word of greeting, Ephraim took her arm, and they began their walk on the road to Tiverton. The darkness of the night enveloped them like a shroud, a harbinger of the secrets that lay concealed.

Sarah's voice trembled with desperation as she asked, "Where are we going?"

"To Durfee's farm," Ephraim replied, "I noticed he had a large stack of hay in his field. We can sit down in the shelter of that and be as comfortable as though we were at the meeting house."

They continued to walk, and Sarah inquired further, "Have you come to any conclusion as to what should be done?"

"Yes, I feel it's the best solution and will solve everything."

Sarah Maria's next question revealed her apprehension: "Well, where shall I go? Have you found a place where no one would be likely to find out?"

Avery's reply sent chills through me. "You need not go away at all."

"But if I stay, I shall be disgraced," Sarah Maria implored, her voice filled with anguish.

Avery's presence grew more sinister, his words tinged with deception. "No! I will fix that."

"How, pray tell, will you do that?"

"Wait until we get to the haystack, and I will tell you," Avery said in a low voice, his true intentions shrouded in darkness.

Avoiding Durfee's house, they reached the haystack, where they seated themselves on the sheltered side.

"Now," she said, her eyes fixed on Avery, "what is your plan?"

He made no immediate reply to her direct question. For several agonizing minutes, he remained silent, as if contemplating the depths of his nefarious scheme. When he finally spoke, his voice was low, a sinister whisper that carried the weight of his malevolent intentions:

"Sarah, you know there is no way I can marry you now, and if the news ever got out that I fathered a bastard child, it would be the end of my ministerial service to God and my congregation. The only way out of this dreadful situation is to let the child go. It is a sacrifice we must make for the good of all involved. We would never want our child to suffer the shame and embarrassment of being a bastard. I have a remedy concocted by the local apothecary that will help you be regular again. Please take it!"

Sarah could not believe what she was hearing. She thought to herself, *This man who has the nerve to call himself a minister of God wants to kill our child.* She screamed at him, "You murderous monster; you will not kill my child! I will not take your poison!"

He responded with a harsh and venomous tone, saying, "You will take the remedy, even if I have to force it down your throat!"

Fearing that the life of her unborn child was in grave danger, she jolted upright and ran towards Farmer Durfee's house as fast as her short legs would let her; however, her stride was no match for his. He quickly overshadowed her and dragged her back to the haystack, her muddied shoes falling off her feet.

The Murder

Ephraim's desperation grew, and he resorted to drastic measures. Pushing Sarah down to the ground, he straddled her chest and arms, pulled the cork, forced her mouth open, and poured the entire contents of the small green bottle down her throat. She thrashed her legs wildly, trying to get Ephraim off her chest, but he overpowered her. He continued to straddle her until he was sure that the abortifacient had done its job.

The vision became increasingly horrifying. Suffering severe pain and distress. She cried out in agony, "Lord, have mercy on me! Ephraim, what have you done? You are killing me and my baby!" Within a few seconds, she lost consciousness. With x-ray vision, I watched as the overdose of abortifacient coursed throughout her body, severely narrowing her blood vessels and, as a result, significantly decreasing the supply of oxygen, not only to her uterus and vital organs but also to her brain, which caused her to lose consciousness. After a few moments of sitting on top of her limp body, thinking that she was in some type of swoon, he looked around for something heavy that he could place on her abdomen to help induce the abortion. On the ground a few feet away was a piece of flagstone, about a foot in diameter. He walked over, picked up the heavy stone, and placed it on her abdomen and upper legs. With the weight of the stone on top of her, Sarah didn't budge.

Fearing that she might be dead, Ephraim quickly devised a plan he hoped would cover his evil deed. In the distance, silhouetted against the horizon, he saw a farm wagon. He ran to it in hopes of finding something that would help him dig a grave. Once there, he didn't find anything that would help him bury her, but he did find several sacks. He picked one up and thought to himself, *This will do just fine. It's hemp and very strong.* With visions in his head of staging her suicide, he unraveled the twine used to sew the large sack together and threw the remnants back into the wagon. He ran back to the haystack with the twine in his hand.

Still unconscious, Sarah's lifeless body was sprawled out on the ground. He removed the stone, lifted her shoulders, pulled her head back, and wrapped the twine around her neck twice. He crossed the ends and tightened the loop with all his force. Sarah reflexively opened her eyes and gasped for air. The twine cut deeply into her flesh. Her body jerked several times, and then she stopped moving. Her hands fell limp by her side, and her head dropped back. With a cold and calculating detachment, he dropped her head to the ground.

The vision continued to unfold like a horror movie, with Avery climbing atop a bail of hay and lifting the limp corpse by the rope he strangled her with. He tied it to a sturdy stake used to contain the hay, and as he raised her petite body, her long, dark hair cascaded down, veiling her sweet face from the unholy gaze of her murderer. After tying her body to the stake, he folded her clothes and placed them along with her shoes neatly under her knees in a grotesque attempt to make it look like she committed suicide.

As my vision continued, Ephraim cast one last look around him, making sure that no prying eyes bore witness to his crime. With the weight of his terrible deed hanging over him like a shroud, he vaulted the fence, his guilty conscience pushing him to flee down the road toward Howland's Bridge.

Sarah's long hair, once a symbol of youth and vitality, now floated back and forth on the night breeze, a mournful dance in the frigid air. The night seemed to stretch on, interminable, as if time itself held its breath, haunted by the tragedy that had unfolded.

Then, in the distance, the first hints of the gray December dawn began to break the oppressive darkness. The feeble light of day, with its somber, muted hues, heralded the coming of morning. It cast its pallid glow upon the spectral scene, illuminating all that remained to bear witness to the terrible deed—the inanimate form of the victim, the chilling tableau of a life unjustly ended, was a bleak reminder of the darkness that can reside within the human soul.

My Reflections on the Vision

At the time the crime was committed, Ephraim Avery was one of the most prominent elders of the Methodist Church, and as a revivalist, he had a reputation as the equal of Moody and Sankey. He seduced Miss Cornell, who was a member of his church, and afterward murdered her and hung the body in a haystack. He was arrested, and although circumstantial evidence was strong against him, his friends determined that he should not be hung and perjured themselves to save him. This murder created great fervor at that time, and even now it is often referred to as the "Terrible Haystack Murder." The date of this awful murder was December 20, 1832.

Sarah is in heaven, and her soul is at rest. She has long forgiven Ephraim Avery and views him as a victim of evil because he could not resist the lust of the flesh. The message she has given me to share is: "We have all fallen short of the glory of God. Choose to love one another. Learn to forgive and trust God."

ABOUT THE AUTHOR

Shirley Smolko, *The Venetian Medium,* is a natural Psychic Medium, which means she was born with the ability to perceive psychic information and communicate with the souls of people that have passed away. In addition to being a Psychic Medium, she is a publisher, author, and lecturer. She holds a Bachelor of Science in Nursing, a Masters in Business Administration, and another Masters degree in the Science of Accounting. She is also certified in grief counseling. Shirley lives in the USA with her husband, Joe, and their two cats—Zoey and Cecilia. You can find out more about Shirley, her books, and what she is up to by going to: venetianmedium.com, or cavallaropub.com.

OTHER BOOKS BY THE AUTHOR

Books By Shirley Smolko (As Of This Printing):

- *My Adventures as a Psychic Nurse & Medium: Spirits Everywhere!* (Previously published as: *Adventures of a Psychic Nurse: Spirits Everywhere!*)
- *My Adventures as a Psychic Nurse & Medium: Haunted Hospital!* (Previously published as: *More Adventures of a Psychic Nurse: Haunted Hospitals!*)
- *Just a Thought Away: Communicating With Loved Ones In Spirit*
- *Money Wants Me!*
- *Money at Your Command!*
- *Secret to the Science of Getting Rich*
- *At Your Command!*
- *Revelations of the Afterlife: A New Arrival*
- Wisdom From the Wealthy Dead: A Medium Interviews the Souls of Three American Tycoons
- Wisdom From the Wealthy Dead: A Medium Interviews the Soul of Andrew Carnegie
- The Murdered Dead Speak: Book I

Be Sure to Look for Even More Books to Come!

www.ingramcontent.com/pod-product-compliance
Lightning Source LLC
Chambersburg PA
CBHW071019120626
46546CB00003B/1165